BAHÁ'U'LLÁH
THE PRINCE OF
PEACE
A Portrait

Verily this is that Most Great Beauty, foretold in the Books of the Messengers, through Whom truth shall be distinguished from error and the wisdom of every command shall be tested. Verily He is the Tree of Life that bringeth forth the fruits of God, the Exalted, the Powerful, the Great.

The time foreordained unto the peoples and kindreds of the earth is now come.

— BAHÁ'U'LLÁH

*he face of him on whom I gazed I can never forget, though I cannot* describe it. Those piercing eyes seemed to read one's very soul; power and authority sat on that ample brow; while the deep lines on the forehead and face implied an age which the jet-black hair and beard flowing down in indistinguishable luxuriance almost to the waist seemed to belie. No need to ask in whose presence I stood, as I bowed myself before one who is the object of a devotion and love which kings might envy and emperors sigh for in vain!

BAHÁ'U'LLÁH

THE PRINCE OF PEACE

A Portrait

by

DAVID HOFMAN

GEORGE RONALD
OXFORD

GEORGE RONALD, Publisher
46 High Street, Kidlington OX5 2DN

British Library Cataloguing in Publication Data

Hofman, David
Baha'u'llah, prince of peace: A portrait.
I. Title
297.092

ISBN 0–85398–338–0
ISBN 0–85398–340–2 Pbk

Printed in Great Britain by
Billing & Sons Ltd, Worcester

CONTENTS

Preface   ix

Introduction   xi

1. Hope for Mankind   1
2. The New Age   6
3. The Bahá'í Peace Programme   10
4. The New Revelation   37
5. The Nobleman of Núr   41
6. Mírzá Ḥusayn-'Alí, the Bábí   48
7. Prisoner in the Síyáh-Chál   53
8. Exile   57
9. Darvísh Muḥammad-i-Írání   64
10. Return to Baghdad   70
11. Bahá'u'lláh's Declaration of His Mission   85
12. By Caravan to Constantinople   92
13. The Third Banishment   99
14. The Proclamation to the Kings and
    Religious Leaders   105
15. Adrianople and the Last Banishment   130
16. 'Akká, the Most Great Prison   146
17. Freedom   167
18. Bahjí – The Final Years   169
19. The Ascension of Bahá'u'lláh   179
Bibliography   183
References   185
Index   191

PREFACE

THE western writer who attempts, with no knowledge of Arabic or Persian, the languages in which His revelation was uttered, to portray Bahá'u'lláh, is not so handicapped as may at first seem. Bahá'u'lláh appointed His eldest son, 'Abdu'l-Bahá, as the Centre of His Covenant, the Interpreter of His revelation, the Head of His Cause, and conferred upon His utterance the same authority as exists in His own. 'Abdu'l-Bahá visited Europe and North America and His many addresses, some thousands of His letters, His 'table talk' to a western enquirer, and His major written works are all available in English.

In His Will and Testament 'Abdu'l-Bahá appointed His eldest grandson, Shoghi Effendi, Guardian of the Cause and devolved upon him the mantle of Interpreter and Expounder of the revelation. Shoghi Effendi's authorized translation into English of the sacred texts is enriched by the vast range of his historical and expository works comprising his World Order essays, his meticulously documented record of the first hundred years of Bahá'í history entitled *God Passes By*, his translation of the first volume of Nabíl-i-A'zam's immortal history of the Bábí Dispensation and his great works *The Advent of Divine Justice* and *The Promised Day is Come* which document the impact of the Bahá'í revelation on the modern world and the shaping of its future development. Shoghi Effendi was not only a descendant of Bahá'u'lláh, Persian and Arabic being his mother tongues, but his study of English began at an early age and continued through his education at Balliol College, Oxford. Everything in his ministry of thirty-six years is the prime source to all Bahá'ís of their knowledge of Bahá'u'lláh and their understanding of His revelation.

The events of Bahá'u'lláh's life are documented in the state records of the European powers, whose consuls in the 19th century were epidemic throughout the Middle East – at that time, the Turkish Empire and Persia. In addition, many western scholars and orientalists have recorded details of and commented on various aspects of Bahá'u'lláh's life and these have been gathered in a project of masterly research by Dr Moojan Momen in his *The Bábí and Bahá'í Religions, 1844–1944: Some Contemporary Western Accounts*. No account of Bahá'u'lláh's life could ever be called definitive, but H. M. Balyuzi's monumental work *Bahá'u'lláh, the King of Glory* must surely be the nearest possible. Adib Taherzadeh's four volumes *The Revelation of Bahá'u'lláh* are a mine of information about the Prophet Himself and His teachings. From all the above sources I have drawn heavily.

To the Universal House of Justice I express loving thanks for constant encouragement in the daunting task and for referring my queries to its Research Department. My old friend and helper Roger White gave me great assistance and encouragement during the early stages of the writing and read the completed typescript, offering his usual perceptive and valuable comments. To Dr Iraj Ayman, Director of Landegg Academy, and his staff and indeed Landegg Academy itself, I owe a debt of special gratitude for warm hospitality in peace and freedom from daily cares enabling me to concentrate on the work. René V. Steiner, Programme Coordinator of the Academy, has used his computer and word processor to transform my surrealist manuscript and continual revisions and amendments into a neat typescript, for which assistance no expression of thanks is adequate.

INTRODUCTION

THIS is the story of Bahá'u'lláh, the Persian nobleman who became a Bábí and thereby forfeited the life of ease and comfort, the high station among men to which He had been born, and embraced vilification, scorn, despoliation, torture, imprisonment and exile for the rest of His life. But He shook the world and initiated the process of the 'rolling up' of the old moribund order of things, and opened to our minds the prospect of a new, world order in which the tyrannies, the cruelty, the injustice, the inhumanity, prejudice and bitter hatreds and hypocrisy of the past would give way to peace and justice, honour and self-respect, love for one God and unity among nations.

His teachings were revolutionary and anathema to the leaders of mankind in the nineteenth century. They paled at the implications of the oneness of mankind, the oneness of religion, the equality of the sexes, the abandonment of dominant empires, the education of all men and women everywhere. To them the idea that 'The earth is but one country and mankind its citizens' was subversion. No armaments! No wars! How could any nation foster its own interests without them? 'Yet so it shall be; these fruitless strifes, these ruinous wars shall pass away, and the "Most Great Peace" shall come.'[1]

So huge a transformation in human life could not possibly

be achieved by one man. Only the power of God could accomplish it. Bahá'u'lláh, as He lay in chains in the Síyáh-Chál – the Black Hole of Teheran – was summoned by the Voice of God and was invested with the authority and power and attributes of God Himself. He became the Bearer of the new revelation from God, the Founder of the long-awaited, Christ-promised Kingdom, the Redeemer of mankind, the Appearance, the Manifestation of God, the Promised One of all ages. 'To Israel He was . . . the incarnation of the "Everlasting Father", the "Lord of Hosts" come down "with ten thousands of saints"; to Christendom Christ returned "in the glory of the Father", to Shí'ah Islám the return of the Imám Husayn; to Sunní Islám the descent of the "Spirit of God" (Jesus Christ); to the Zoroastrians the promised Sháh-Bahrám; to the Hindus the reincarnation of Krishna; to the Buddhists the fifth Buddha.'[2]

The life of a Manifestation of God does not admit of normal biographical treatment. Who shall assess or evaluate or presume to discuss the inner reality of Christ, of Buddha, of Muhammad? That exalted Being is the greatest mystery, more mysterious even than God Himself, Whom we accept perforce as unknowable, single and alone. But His revealer dwells among us. His body is susceptible to all the vicissitudes of human life and He accepts for Himself whatever treatment the world offers Him. Indeed the appearance of that divine Being 'in the noble form of the human temple' is one of the clouds upon which He descends, the dark veil which conceals His splendour from all but the pure in heart, who 'shall see God'. We may no longer gaze, like Professor Browne, upon His person 'with a throb of wonder and awe', but we can, by consideration of His message and the sublimity of His life, apprehend the grand redemptive scheme of God which He unfolds and gaze with awe and wonder upon the majesty and grandeur with which He admonishes the kings and rulers of the world and takes upon His shoulder the government of mankind.

Bahá'u'lláh, outwardly, was a captive of the two most despotic rulers of the age — the Shah and the Sultan. He languished in their prisons, suffered their tortures, endured their banishments, but He conquered them both and all who opposed Him. He opened a new vision to men's hearts and minds. Thousands gave their life's blood in His service, and ever more thousands have raised His banner in all parts of the earth and in the midmost heart of the ocean, where, in Samoa a Bahá'í House of Worship proclaims the Day of God across the vast Pacific.

For the easier reading and better understanding of His story it is helpful to consider the illumination which He sheds upon the reality of the Manifestation of God. He speaks in two voices: 'I am but a man like you', and 'Before Abraham was I am'. The point is well illustrated in an anecdote about Muhammad. One day He consulted His companions about an idea and they asked Him whether it was His own or from God. He replied that if it had been from God He would not have consulted them. All power and authority is given to that holy one, but He is not God. In one of His prayers Bahá'u'llah revealed

When I contemplate, O my God, the relationship that bindeth me to Thee, I am moved to proclaim to all created things 'verily I am God!'; and when I consider my own self, lo, I find it coarser than clay![3]

We know God through His Manifestations; all else is what we imagine. The Manifestation reveals God to us, 'whoso hath seen Me hath seen the Father', but He is not that 'innermost Spirit of Spirits', that 'eternal Essence of Essences' the unknowable Creator who has brought us into being out of nothingness. This truth is vital to the abolition of religious prejudice and the recognition of one God. The subject is dealt with in greater detail in Chapter 3. It is mentioned now to clarify that when Bahá'u'lláh speaks with the voice of God He does so with the authority conferred on Him in the Síyáh-

Chál, as Jesus spoke with the authority conferred upon Him through the dove, or Moses through the voice from the burning bush, or Muhammad through the Angel Gabriel who commanded Him to 'cry in the name of Thy Lord'.

Fortunately, the events of Bahá'u'lláh's life (1817–92) are accessible to us from authentic sources, His writings and records of contemporaries. The historical facts are documented in state archives, and the effects of His teachings are for all to see in the rise of a worldwide community bearing His name and dedicated to the full implementation of the central theme of His revelation, the oneness of mankind.* The principles which He enunciated a hundred years ago, considered revolutionary or utopian at the time, have now, by their worldwide diffusion and perspicuous relevance to the current situation, become the *sine qua non* of a modern outlook.

This story of Bahá'u'lláh tells of magnificent heroism, nobility, stark evil, cruelty and betrayal and of the victory of God. We enter the realm of kings and queens, governors of provinces and cities, high priests and politicians, diplomats and soldiers, popular demonstrations, intimations of the onrushing forces of social change and the disintegration of a moribund and 'lamentably defective' system of world relationships. We perceive the unfolding of a wonderful vision of a spiritually unified humanity, God-conscious, God-orientated, God-intoxicated, secure in the realms of its Almighty and Everlasting Father under the reign of the Lord of Hosts, the King of Kings, the Prince of Peace.

---

* 1988 *Britannica Book of the Year* lists in its section on the dispersion of the world religions, the Bahá'í Faith at this date, less than 100 years after the ascension of its founder, as second only to Christianity.

Chapter 1

HOPE FOR MANKIND

THERE is no more urgent or intractable problem facing mankind today than the establishment of peace in the world. This is no longer a dream of visionaries or an expression of vague and pious hope but the essential prerequisite to the continuance of human life on this planet. But no brake has yet been devised to stem the headlong acceleration towards disaster, and the fear of a nuclear holocaust is ever with us.

The huge disturbance now engulfing the planet is clear evidence of a sickness at the heart of humanity which the greatest efforts of statesmen and leaders are unable to diagnose or allay. The breakdown is not limited to the political sphere but affects every department of human life, reaching down to the family and individuals. Man's basic activities turn against him: his sectarian religions, divisive politics, destructive industry, selfish economics, debased arts; his stubborn clinging to outworn shibboleths of national sovereignty and racial superiority, together with a cancerous materialism and cynical heedlessness of his own spiritual nature, imperil his very life.

The dramatic emergence of the Bahá'í Faith onto the world stage has been precipitated by frequent recurrences in recent years of the savage persecution with which it was greeted in Iran, the land of its birth. During its short history — less than one hundred and fifty years — many assaults have been made on the lives, property, dignity and very existence of the Bahá'í community in that country. The latest outbreak in 1979–90 bore all the evidences of a planned and ruthless programme of extermination.

This time, however, owing to the rapid spread of the Faith and the rise of its administrative institutions throughout the world, it was able to mobilize its defences and call to the attention of governments, international organizations and the media – all concerned as never before with human rights and freedom – every specific act of the fanatical Shi'ah clergy against the harassed community, acts ranging from destruction of its holy places to the torture and execution of men, women and children who would not recant their faith in exchange for life and liberty.

What is this Bahá'í Faith and who is Baha'u'lláh, its founder? Whence comes its power to inspire in the members of a decadent nation such steadfast heroism as to recall the early martyrs of Christianity and Islam? By what magic does it change the darkness of their ignorance and superstition into a world-embracing outlook higher than anything which humanity as a whole has as yet conceived and of which it stands, at this very moment, in such dire need?

The increasing disruption of the old order of the world has led to a widespread conviction that we are entering a new period of human history. Thoughtful people realize that this worldwide agitation is no transitory dislocation, childhood sickness or adolescent fever. It signifies an organic change in the nature of human life on earth, a change such as we associate with the coming of age in individuals, and which must surely have its counterpart in the collective life of mankind and the organization of the planet. Humanity is coming of age and is beset with all the disruption, instability and confusion experienced by individuals as they come into full possession of their physical, mental and spiritual powers.

This period of instability, unless we are to destroy all life on our planet, can have only one outcome – the precipitation of a world society. Out of the confusion, pain and labour of our time, world order is being born, opening to mankind the portals of a new era of peace, brotherhood and happiness.

Such a consummation has been the dream and hope of peoples, the vision of poets, the promise of religions from the beginning of recorded history. It has been characterized as the Day of God, the Kingdom of God on earth, the New Jerusalem, or such, and has been associated in all religions with the coming of a divine messenger, or the return of each one's founder, the Promised One of all ages.

Bahá'u'lláh announced Himself as that one and His message the promised revelation of truth upon which will be founded that Kingdom: 'O concourse of the rulers and of the learned and the wise! The Promised Day is come and the Lord of Hosts hath appeared. Rejoice ye with great joy by reason of this supreme felicity.'[1]

But He clearly foresaw the chaos and confusion of our times and in emphatic statements warned the kings and rulers of the day of what was to come:

The world is in travail and its agitation waxeth day by day. Its face is turned towards waywardness and unbelief.[2]

How long will humanity persist in its waywardness? How long will injustice continue? How long is chaos and confusion to reign amongst men? How long will discord agitate the face of society? The winds of despair are, alas, blowing from every direction, and the strife that divides and afflicts the human race is daily increasing. The signs of impending convulsions and chaos can now be discerned, inasmuch as the prevailing order appears to be lamentably defective.[3]

Soon will the present-day order be rolled up, and a new one spread out in its stead.[4]

Bahá'u'lláh made it clear that world peace would not be brought about by any sudden magical act but by the response of mankind to the new message from God of which He was the bearer. The maturity of mankind demands its unity, and man will not be mature until he attains that unity. 'The well-being of mankind,' He declares, 'its peace and security, are unattainable unless and until its unity is firmly established.'[5]

Fortunately it is not left to human wisdom to define the principles and control the forces which will bring to fruition the tree of human existence. Man is a spiritual being, dependent for his knowledge of spiritual laws and spiritual truth on great spiritual teachers. He has never discovered spiritual truth for himself as he discovers physical truth through research and experiment. The 'commandments' of Moses have never been superseded and are still the foundation of social order while it is the teachings and influence of Moses, Jesus, Buddha, Muhammad, Zoroaster and Krishna which have formulated the morals and ethical standards of the great civilizations. Not scientific knowledge, not technology, military power, education, social welfare; we have all these today in greater array than ever before, but the confusion in the world and the danger to life increase daily.

Man is starving for spiritual knowledge, unable to perceive his own true nature, yet trying to harness the majestic powers of maturity to the moribund social, economic, political systems of childhood. The spiritual force of the principle embodied in the words of Bahá'u'lláh 'the earth is but one country and mankind its citizens' is shaking to bits the ramshackle old contraption of competing enemy states, precariously balanced on the tightrope of such moribund and obsolescent doctrines as unfettered national sovereignty, relentless economic competition, racial and class prejudices, bitterly antagonistic religious systems. 'This is a new cycle of human power,' 'Abdu'l-Bahá announced in the City Temple in London on September 10th, 1911. 'All the horizons of the world are luminous, and the world will become indeed as a garden and a paradise. It is the hour of unity of the sons of men and of the drawing together of all races and all classes. You are loosed from ancient superstitions which have kept men ignorant, destroying the foundation of true humanity.'[6]

Chapter 2

THE NEW AGE

THE magnificent nineteenth century witnessed the transformation of human life from a stagnating, devitalized uninspiring set of formulas, to a furious activity in every aspect of life on the planet, a furore not yet abating, but culminating in the dislocation, terror and confusion of this day. It was indeed the watershed of human development.

At the turn of the century the hopes raised by the French Revolution, which, as Carlyle put it, befittingly terminated the falsity of the eighteenth century, quickly gave way to disillusionment as the ideals of liberty, brotherhood and equality seemed to be as far off as ever. But there were new forces at work in the world. The false dawn was followed by a true one. The adventism of the first half of the century which erupted at various points throughout the religious communities of the world, all of which had expectation of the coming of a Messiah, was no fortuitous coincidence, but the first stirrings of the new springtime.

The wonderful romantic movement, far from being confined to literature and the two or three decades usually assigned to it, expressed the unconscious anticipation by the human spirit of the coming dawn, and extended far beyond Europe and the early nineteenth century into other continents and the objective worlds of politics and social order. The Shaykhi movement,[1] emerging in Persia at the end of the eighteenth century, and Robert Burns's ringing cry for human brotherhood, may be regarded as two of its earliest manifestations. Tennyson, living until 1892, penned the famous lines:

> Till the war-drum throbb'd no longer, and the battle-flags were furl'd
> In the Parliament of man, the Federation of the world. [2]

And it was well into the twentieth century when the world vision of Woodrow Wilson begot the League of Nations and infused into world politics, however tentatively, the concept of one ordered world.

In the west the industrial revolution was under way. Men who had lived with the same tools and scarcely greater sources of energy than were available to the Romans or Chaldeans began to discover the powers of steam and electricity, to apply them with growing ingenuity to technical devices for production and communication. The first public railway line was opened in 1830; the first telegram was sent on May 24th, 1844. The aborted ideals of the French Revolution came alive again and a brilliant array of social reformers lit up the sky of the middle century. Wilberforce, Lincoln, Shaftesbury and Fry and a host of others worked to ameliorate man's inhumanity to man. Slavery was made illegal in one country after another, child labour was abolished, factory acts were passed to make the lot of workers more humane, prison reforms were undertaken, education became universal and compulsory, and newspapers achieved popular circulation. Africa and the Pacific Ocean were explored and the mapping of the entire planet was initiated; world languages were invented and the emancipation of women began; and so the story continued. Medicine, music, the arts and social life, every activity of man was caught up in the huge explosion.

This new knowledge and enterprise were not matched by comparable advances in spiritual perception. In spite of a growing humanitarianism, belief in God and religious faith suffered serious decline as the portraits of the universe offered by the religious establishments were seen to be less and less in conformity with the truly wonderful and astonishing reality uncovered by science. Religious leaders clung to their literal, physical and often naive interpretations of spiritual teachings with the inevitable result that a general disillusionment with the relevance of religious truth to reality and therefore to practical affairs supervened. It led to widespread agnosticism and atheism, leaving humanity without spiritual guidance or ultimate moral sanction and rendering it incapable of managing the enormous powers increasingly placed at its disposal. This is the present situation.

Bahá'u'lláh's comment on the spiritual condition of the late nineteenth century was

The vitality of men's belief in God is dying out in every land; nothing short of His wholesome medicine can ever restore it. The corrosion of ungodliness is eating into the vitals of human society; what else but the Elixir of His potent Revelation can cleanse and revive it?[3]

Nineteen hundred years previously Jesus the Christ had foretold the same condition, as recorded in the twenty-fourth chapter of St Matthew. When asked about His future coming and the end of the age He replied that it would be attended by

wars and rumours of wars . . . nation shall rise against nation and kingdom against kingdom . . . there shall be famines, and pestilences, and earthquakes, in divers places . . . many false prophets shall rise, and shall deceive many . . . iniquity shall abound, the love of many shall wax cold . . . For then shall be great tribulation, such as was not since the beginning of the world to this time, no, nor ever shall be.

Perusal of the daily newspapers or hearing any regular bulletin of world news provide ample support for the proposition that the time foretold has come. We are living in it now.

As Jesus likened this time to 'the abomination of desolation spoken by Daniel the prophet', so Bahá'u'lláh, a hundred years ago, wrote of it, 'Such shall be its plight that to disclose it now would not be meet and seemly.'[4]

In spite of the ending of the cold war and the remarkable events taking place in Europe, the immediate outlook is dark. But the pains which our generation must endure are the birth pangs of world order – the opening of a new era in history, not its death throes.

Professor Browne is the only westerner known to have left an account of an interview with Bahá'u'lláh. Published in *A Traveller's Narrative*, it is partially quoted as the frontispiece of this book, and contains the following: 'A mild dignified voice bade me be seated, and then continued:

Praise be to God that thou hast attained! . . . Thou has come to see a prisoner and an exile . . . We desire but the good of the world and the happiness of the nations; yet they deem us a stirrer-up of strife and sedition worthy of bondage and banishment . . . That all nations should become one in faith and all men as brothers; that the bonds of affection and unity between the sons of men should be strengthened; that diversity of religion should cease, and differences of race be annulled – what harm is there in this? . . . Yet so it shall be; these fruitless strifes, these ruinous wars shall pass away, and the Most Great Peace shall come . . . Do not you in Europe need this also? Is not this that which Christ foretold? . . . Yet do we see your kings and rulers lavishing their treasures more freely on means for the destruction of the human race than on that which would conduce to the happiness of mankind. These strifes and this bloodshed and discord must cease and all men be as one kindred and one family. Let not a man glory in this, that he loves his country; let him rather glory in this, that he loves his kind.

Browne comments, 'Such, so far as I can recall them, were the words which, besides many others, I heard from Bahá. Let those who read them consider well within themselves whether such doctrines merit death and bonds, and whether the world is more likely to gain or lose by their diffusion.'[5]

Chapter 3

THE BAHÁ'Í PEACE
PROGRAMME

BEFORE describing the measures which Bahá'u'lláh has prescribed for the establishment of peace in the world, it is necessary to consider two essential overriding factors without which the 'Most Great Peace' will not be achieved. These two prime requisites are universal recognition of the oneness of mankind and the oneness of religion. Bahá'u'lláh declared,

The well-being of mankind, its peace and security, are unattainable unless and until its unity is firmly established.

while in His Tablet to Queen Victoria He wrote,

That which the Lord hath ordained as the sovereign remedy and mightiest instrument for the healing of all the world is the union of all its peoples in one universal Cause, one common Faith. This can in no wise be achieved except through the power of a skilled, an all-powerful and inspired Physician.[1]

The accomplishment of these basic requirements implies so vast a transformation in every aspect of human life that Bahá'u'lláh envisaged it in two steps which He named the Lesser Peace and the Most Great Peace, the former designed to abolish war and pave the way for the spiritualization, the regeneration, the re-education of the entire world and its reorganization in that Christ-promised Kingdom of God on earth which is the Most Great Peace.

The Peace brought to the world by Bahá'u'lláh, although in its initial stage bolstered by treaties and international covenants, agreed delineation of borders and the firm application of the principle of collective security, in its mature development goes far beyond such considerations which must surely come to be regarded as the firm voice of law and order controlling an unruly class of adolescents. There is a vast difference between the Lesser Peace and the Most Great Peace. The former may be attained whenever the nations, under the leadership of the super-powers, summon up the will to do it. Recent events clearly foreshadow the coming event, which may well take place before the end of the century. The latter requires the skill of 'an all-powerful and inspired Physician' to prescribe the remedies for the sick body of mankind.

God hath verily purposed to bring the hearts of men together, though it require every means on earth and in the heavens.[2]

The Lesser Peace

Having announced to the kings and rulers and religious leaders of the late nineteenth century the message entrusted to Him by God,* and having received only disdain, enmity, persecution, torture, imprisonment and banishment, He addressed again, in that same Tablet to Queen Victoria, 'the concourse of the rulers of the earth':

Now that ye have refused the Most Great Peace, hold ye fast unto this, the Lesser Peace, that haply ye may in some degree better your own condition and that of your dependents.

. . . Be reconciled among yourselves, that ye may need no more armaments save in a measure to safeguard your territories and dominions . . .

Be united, O kings of the earth, for thereby will the tempest of discord be stilled amongst you, and your peoples find rest, if ye be

* See Chapter 14.

of them that comprehend. Should any one among you take up arms against another, rise ye all against him, for this is naught but manifest justice.[3]

Thus was communicated to mankind the principle of collective security, long before governments and political leaders had envisaged or considered it. In many passages of His writings Bahá'u'lláh stressed it and urged its implementation:

The Great Being, wishing to reveal the prerequisites of the peace and tranquillity of the world and the advancement of its peoples, hath written: The time must come when the imperative necessity for the holding of a vast, an all-embracing assemblage of men will be universally realized. The rulers and kings of the earth must needs attend it, and participating in its deliberations, must consider such ways and means as will lay the foundations of the world's Great Peace amongst men. Such a peace demandeth that the Great Powers should resolve, for the sake of the tranquillity of the peoples of the earth, to be fully reconciled among themselves. Should any king take up arms against another, all should unitedly arise and prevent him. If this be done, the nations of the world will no longer require any armaments, except for the purpose of preserving the security of their realms and of maintaining internal order within their territories. This will ensure the peace and composure of every people, government and nation.[4]

'Abdu'l-Bahá, elaborating this theme, wrote:

True civilization will unfurl its banner in the midmost heart of the world whenever a certain number of its distinguished and high-minded sovereigns — the shining exemplars of devotion and determination — shall, for the good and happiness of all mankind, arise, with firm resolve and clear vision, to establish the Cause of Universal Peace. They must make the Cause of Peace the object of general consultation, and seek by every means in their power to establish a Union of the nations of the world. They must conclude a binding treaty and establish a covenant, the provisions of which shall be sound, inviolable and definite. They must proclaim it to all the world and obtain for it the sanction of all the human race. This supreme and noble undertaking — the real source of the peace and well-being of all the world — should be regarded as sacred by all that dwell on earth. All the forces of humanity must be mobilized to ensure the stability and permanence of this Most Great Covenant. In this all-embracing Pact the limits and frontiers of each and every nation should be clearly fixed, the principles underlying the relations of governments towards one another definitely laid down, and all international agreements and obligations ascertained. In like manner, the size of the armaments of every government should be strictly limited, for if the preparations for war and the military forces of any nation should be allowed to increase, they will arouse the suspicion of others. The fundamental principle underlying this solemn Pact should be so fixed that if any government later violate any one of its provisions, all the governments on earth should arise to reduce it to utter submission, nay the human race as a whole should resolve, with every power at its disposal, to destroy that government. Should this greatest of all remedies be applied to the sick body of the world, it will assuredly recover from its ills and will remain eternally safe and secure.[5]

Shoghi Effendi,* in his essay *The Goal of a New World Order* (1931), set forth the immediate implications of these counsels:

What else could these weighty words signify if they did not point to the inevitable curtailment of unfettered national sovereignty as an indispensable preliminary to the formation of the future Commonwealth of all the nations of the world? Some form of a world Super-State must needs be evolved, in whose favour all the nations of the world will have willingly ceded every claim to make war, certain rights to impose taxation and all rights to maintain armaments, except for purposes of maintaining internal order within their respective dominions. Such a state will have to include within its orbit an International Executive adequate to enforce supreme and unchallengeable authority on every recalcitrant member of the commonwealth . . .[6]

The pathetic and timorous efforts of world leaders after the establishment of the League of Nations to curb in any degree the claims of 'unfettered national sovereignty' — adamantly maintained whilst paying lip service to the ideals of the League — had no restraining effect on the rake's progress towards

* See Preface.

World War II. Even after that appalling tragedy, no such supra-national authority as is envisioned by Bahá'u'lláh has been established, although the United Nations shows great promise. The nations cling to their moribund, 'outworn shibboleths of national creeds',[7] the philosophy internationally of the pirate and the brigand. No national government permits its cities, towns and villages to maintain armaments 'save as a measure to safeguard their territories', that is, a police force subject to the law. The formation of some world authority with power to say, 'No! Stop it!' to any national government is the sole hope for bringing about the Lesser Peace.

In October 1985 the Universal House of Justice – the world head of the Bahá'í Faith – published a booklet entitled *The Promise of World Peace*. Its publication was timed to coincide with the fortieth anniversary of the founding of the United Nations. It was addressed to 'The Peoples of the World' and has had, and is having, a remarkable circulation. It has been presented to the Secretary-General of the United Nations, most Heads of State, Prime Ministers and Heads of Government, a great number of members of the world's legislatures, the diplomatic corps, and hundreds of thousands of responsible people in all fields of human endeavour, in all parts of the world. At present it is published in fifty languages. It opens with this uplifting statement:

The Great Peace towards which people of good will throughout the centuries have inclined their hearts, of which seers and poets for countless generations have expressed their vision, and for which from age to age the sacred scriptures of mankind have constantly held the promise, is now at long last within the reach of the nations. For the first time in history it is possible for everyone to view the entire planet, with all its myriad diversified peoples, in one perspective. World peace is not only possible but inevitable. It is the next stage in the evolution of this planet – in the words of one great thinker, 'the planetization of mankind'.[8]*

---

* Teilhard de Chardin.

Towards the end of its message the House of Justice, referring to Bahá'u'lláh's call for 'a vast, an all-embracing assemblage', made this moving appeal:

The holding of this mighty convocation is long overdue.

With all the ardour of our hearts, we appeal to the leaders of all nations to seize this opportune moment and take irreversible steps to convoke this world meeting. All the forces of history impel the human race towards this act which will mark for all time the dawn of its long-awaited maturity.

Will not the United Nations, with the full support of its membership, rise to the high purposes of such a crowning event?

Let men and women, youth, and children everywhere recognize the eternal merit of this imperative action for all peoples and lift up their voices in willing assent. Indeed, let it be this generation that inaugurates this glorious stage in the evolution of social life on the planet.[9]

The persistence of governments in their refusal to cede their so-called sovereign rights to a world federal body has a doubly destructive effect. The international armaments race becomes ever more intense, sabotaging the world's economy, and the illegal use of force makes deeper and deeper inroads into once orderly societies. Rebellion, *coups d'état* and blatant terrorism become increasing features of life in the late twentieth century.

The opening years of the final decade of this most remarkable century have astonished the world by apparently sudden movements within mankind towards those very objectives set out by Bahá'u'lláh in His counsel to the governments and leaders. The heads of the two chief super-powers and many of their ministers have begun to talk of world order; the failure and abandonment of communism in its originating country and throughout Eastern Europe bring to an end the cult of one of the three false gods* enumerated by Shoghi Effendi, which have brought such untold suffering and misery to their wretched worshippers; the ending of the cold war is precipitating the reduction of armaments called for by the Lesser

* The other two are racism and nationalism.

Peace; the long-awaited assumption of authority by the United Nations Security Council, and its direct instruction to an aggressor, however short of Bahá'u'lláh's counsel 'all should unitedly arise', is a major and historic step towards the security of the Lesser Peace; the response of one party in the bygone cold war to the desperate needs of the other party is a bright gleam among the black clouds of world politics, while the concerted movements towards a federated Europe clearly reflect the revolution which has taken place in outlook and attitude since the beginning of the century when that very concept was laughed to scorn.

The world is moving on, propelled by the unseen and unacknowledged power of God operating through Bahá'u'lláh, towards its destined beatitude in the realization of the brotherhood of man, God's Kingdom in the hearts of men and in their social order. Like the sun, Bahá'u'lláh is both the destroyer of the winter of the old, 'lamentably defective' order and the promoter of the new springtime of mankind's maturity:

The world's equilibrium hath been upset through the vibrating influence of this most great, this new World Order. Mankind's ordered life hath been revolutionized through the agency of this unique, this wondrous System – the like of which mortal eyes have never witnessed.[10]

But also:

The Call of God, when raised, breathed a new life into the body of mankind, and infused a new spirit into the whole creation. It is for this reason that the world hath been moved to its depths, and the hearts and consciences of men been quickened.[11]

In the remaining years of this century there are doubtless more and greater events ready to unfold as man reaches his coming of age. However much the two processes overlap, the culmination of the 'rolling up' of the old order must precede the final 'spreading out' of the new one. Intimations of the disruption which may well attend the establishment of the Lesser Peace are already discerned.

The unemployment resulting from the reduction of arms, just begun, must reach huge proportions as the world's armaments industries close down. The millions discharged from the armies, navies and air forces will swell this vast number, while the pressure of under-developed populations demanding justice and a fair apportionment of wealth will add yet more confusion to the universal disruption. At the same time the rigid self-interest displayed by the nations, unable to view the world's economy as a cooperative undertaking, render suspect the occasional but heartwarming references to world order. Are they merely rhetorical or do they portend an insight and an unexpressed determination to pursue that unpalatable but God-given objective? In any case the establishment of the Lesser Peace, now being forced upon the nations by expedience – the handmaid of social evolution – will inevitably precipitate the reorganization of the world into a single order, 'organically unified in all the essential aspects of its life, its political machinery, its spiritual aspiration, its trade and finance, its script and language, and yet infinite in the diversity of the national characteristics of its federated units'. [12]

In other words, unity – not uniformity.

The Lesser Peace will greatly promote the most favourable conditions for the necessary transformation of current attitudes, conventions, assumptions – all that is summed up in the term mores – to a world outlook. The huge wave of gratitude and hope which will surge from billions of human hearts when it is recognized that war is really and truly ended must release such a power into human affairs as no obscurantism, die-hard prejudice or bigotry could resist. It will be easy to like our fellow men and to want for them what we want for ourselves. Nor will such a resurgence of love be left to evaporate into thin air. Mankind's long struggle towards maturity has in itself laid a foundation of world relationships. In scientific exploration, trade, arts, international agreements such as the Postal Union and the law of the sea, international travel, radio waveband allocations, diplomatic conventions and, more recently, in the patient work of the United Nations' agencies and the emergence of international relief and human rights organizations, the sinews of a world society have been growing. Logistically all is possible. Every member of the human race could today be fed, clothed, sheltered, educated and given medical attention. Famines could be averted, the results of natural disasters minimized, damage to the planet could be prevented, if only there were an international, supra-national authority to plan and implement these programmes.

The Lesser Peace will confer this essential institution upon the world, a bounty at least equal to the abolition of war. For no solutions to the major problems of our times are possible without a supra-national authority able to control the assertion of unbridled national sovereignty.

In the Lesser Peace, many of the intractable problems facing the human race today may be solved through the operation of international plans and agencies directed by international authority. But peace of the heart, which is the universal characteristic of the Most Great Peace, will only be achieved by man turning again to God, abandoning his current idols, finding out who he is and striving with joy and concentration of all the forces of his soul to win those supernal gifts which his loving Creator has stored up for him at the time of his coming of age.

The Most Great Peace

'The Kingdom of heaven is within you' is just as true today and forever as when Jesus taught it. The foundation of peace is in the human heart, whence it will spread out to all mankind.

As with everything to do with man, the solution to all his problems is spiritual. Bahá'u'lláh states that the first effulgence from the Book of God

is that man should know his own self and recognize that which leadeth unto loftiness or lowliness, glory or abasement, wealth or poverty. Having attained the stage of fulfilment and reached his maturity, man standeth in need of wealth, and such wealth as he acquireth through crafts or professions is commendable and praiseworthy in the estimation of men of wisdom, and especially in the eyes of servants who dedicate themselves to the education of the world and to the edification of its peoples.[13]

A world economy is essential to a world society. Bahá'u'lláh does not lay down any detailed system of world economics but does prescribe a few basic principles which economists may mould into a world pattern which would ameliorate the struggle for existence, lessen the huge gap between destitution and inordinate personal wealth, remove the constant recurrent crises in the world's economy and provide a just and satisfying distribution of the vast wealth available to man's cooperative ingenuity.

Bahá'u'lláh's economic principles include the following:

- The greatest achievements of science and technology should be available to everyone.

- All must work: no idle rich, no idle poor.

- Limitations of wealth and poverty: a basic minimum standard of living below which no one should recede and limitation of individual wealth. We may comment on this that no individual should have to spend long hours of toil in return for an inadequate subsistence for himself and his dependents; no individual should be burdened with the administration and worry of inordinate wealth. Human beings were created for higher and nobler pursuits. Degrees of wealth are necessary and must be maintained.

- The contest between capital and labour could be solved by all employees receiving, in addition to agreed wages, shares in the company for which they work. They would then become part owners and strikes would be obviated.

Beyond these practical considerations which may inspire

economists to devise good housekeeping arrangements for a
world society, Bahá'u'lláh has elevated every individual's
contribution to the work of the world to the status of worship
of God. This vision of the human race, rising every day, first
to remember God and pray and then to set about the day's
work with a zeal impelled by the knowledge that dedication
to that work is worship of God, is beyond the imagination of
twentieth century minds to conceive. Yet so it shall be, for
the power of the Holy Spirit will accomplish it.

The Lesser Peace must not only calm the raging fury of the
present time but must pave the way for the initiation of those
processes which will, with the help of God, eventually and
inevitably lead to the Most Great Peace. In His reply to a letter
which the Executive Committee of the Central Organization
for a Durable Peace, The Hague, wrote to Him during World
War I, 'Abdu'l-Bahá pointed out that world peace was not a
simple or a single subject, and that if they concentrated solely
on the cessation of fighting, they could not achieve more than
a temporary result. He referred them to Bahá'u'lláh's teachings
on universal peace, given 'fifty years ago' and sent to 'the great
sovereigns of the world'. He enumerated, with comment,
many other considerations which would fill out the structure
of the Most Great Peace.[14]

Education is a vital part of the Bahá'í peace programme —
education, universal and compulsory. A universal curriculum
must contain some obligatory items and also be adaptable to
differing needs. For instance, everyone must learn two languages,
the mother tongue and an international language to be chosen
from among the existing ones or a new one to be invented.
Reading and writing in both will not only preserve local
culture and the rich literatures of the world, but use of the
universal language will greatly help to demolish age-old
barriers to friendship and understanding and to foster a sense
of world citizenship. The oneness of mankind must be taught
in all the schools of the world; likewise the nature of man and
'those things which lead to loftiness and honour', the eternal

verities of religion. Not the creeds and rituals and invented dogmas and doctrines, but reverence for God, uprightness, truthfulness, honesty, trustworthiness, fortitude, courtesy and modesty, all those divine characteristics which are at such discount today. Bahá'u'lláh's Tablet *Words of Paradise* contains the following:

Schools must first train the children in the principles of religion, so that the Promise and the Threat recorded in the Books of God may prevent them from the things forbidden and adorn them with the mantle of the commandments; but this in such a measure that it may not injure the children by resulting in ignorant fanaticism and bigotry.[15]

With the will to do it and with funds available from former defence budgets it would be possible to eliminate illiteracy by the end of this century and instil into new generations the elements of good character.

Bahá'u'lláh disclosed three essential unities which embrace and sustain all those principles which constitute World Order, the final shape of mankind's ordered life on this planet. Within that Order humanity may make infinite progress, towards the image of God individually and the Kingdom of God socially. Both processes envision a never-ending refinement of the soul of man as he penetrates ever more deeply the mystery of his own nature and his society reflects ever more brilliantly the grandeur, the vitality, the felicity of the Most Great Peace.

The three unities stressed by Bahá'u'lláh are

The oneness of God

The oneness of mankind

The oneness of religion

About the first unity there can be little or no discussion. If God exists there is only one. If there were more neither would be God. Men's ideas and concepts inevitably vary – *Quot homines tot sententiae* – but these do not affect the reality of the First Cause, the Primal Will, the Pre-Existent Creator.

About the second and third unities there is a great deal of misapprehension, disunity, conflict, prejudice, bitterness and all uncharitableness. Yet Bahá'u'lláh has been able to inculcate in His followers an abiding and joyful recognition of them both. As His Cause grows in numbers and influence there is hope that the most inveterate barriers to human unity may be overcome, not alone by dread of the dire consequences which result from persistence in them, but more positively by the increasing spread of the knowledge of divine love, poured out in overflowing measure by Bahá'u'lláh as attested by the sufferings which He willingly accepted and the infinite compassion of His revelation. He wrote that He had

consented to be bound with chains that mankind may be released from its bondage, and hath accepted to be made a prisoner within this most mighty Stronghold that the whole world may attain unto true liberty. He hath drained to its dregs the cup of sorrow, that all the peoples of the earth may attain unto abiding joy, and be filled with gladness. This is of the mercy of your Lord, the Compassionate, the Most Merciful. We have accepted to be abased, O believers in the Unity of God, that ye may be exalted, and have suffered manifold afflictions that ye might prosper and flourish.[16]

The Oneness of Mankind

Bahá'u'lláh's statement of the oneness of mankind, the central theme of His revelation, has encountered the same antagonism, prejudice and ingrained obscurantism as has met the statement of every truth whose time has come. Universal, deep-seated, persistent denunciation and unbelief have greeted Bahá'u'lláh's simple statement, 'Ye are all the leaves of one tree'.

This basic axiom is rendered the more unpalatable to the male-dominated religious and social establishments of the planet by two correlative principles enunciated by Bahá'u'lláh. The equality of the sexes and the harmony of religion and science are integral features of the oneness of mankind. 'Man', 'mankind', 'men' are generic terms in Bahá'í terminology, embracing every member of the human race, man, woman and child, past, present and future.

The principle of the equality of men and women heals the age-old schizophrenia which has wrought such misery among half the human race and effectively retarded the ordering and governance of the world. The built-up force of this frustration has burst forth in our day with the power of an explosion with all its attendant violence and excesses. The emancipation of women has yet to be welcomed by the dominant male, and daily life adjusted to meet the requirements of difference of function and equality of status. Until this is achieved the unity of mankind is a chimera.

The principle of the harmony of religion and science comes at a time when the revolution in the historical attitude has come half circle and the ancient dominance of religion has given way to that of science. The oracle and the priest are no longer the sources of wisdom and knowledge; science and scientists have taken over. There is great need for restoration of the balance, but not between scientists and bishops, rather between scientific knowledge and spiritual truth, the two aspects of knowledge.

The vitality of men's belief in God is dying out in every land; nothing short of His wholesome medicine can ever restore it. The corrosion of ungodliness is eating into the vitals of human society; what else but the Elixir of His potent Revelation can cleanse and revive it?[17]

The relevance of this admonition to recent events in Europe is apparent in the collapse and abandonment of communism, an ideology exalted in many of its aspirations but doomed to failure by its rejection of the rock foundation on which social order must be built – the unifying power and discipline of religion. Bahá'u'lláh lays great stress on this:

Religion is verily the chief instrument for the establishment of order in the world and of tranquillity amongst its peoples. The weakening of the pillars of religion hath strengthened the foolish and emboldened them and made them more arrogant. Verily I say: The greater the decline of religion, the more grievous the waywardness of the ungodly. This cannot but lead in the end to chaos and confusion. Hear Me, O men of insight, and be warned, ye who are endued with discernment![18]

Addressing a gathering in New York in 1912 'Abdu'l-Bahá said, 'Science cannot create amity and fellowship in human hearts.'[19] No ideologies, no projects of liberty, equality, fraternity, no institutions of a welfare state are proof against 'the corrosion of ungodliness'. But science and religion together can build the Kingdom of God on earth.

Modern science has clearly proved the oneness of mankind. Anatomy knows only one human structure – infinite in its varieties of size, proportion and hue. Physiology the same – we are all subject to the same process of growth from infancy to the grave, to the needs of food, clothing, shelter, sleep and activity. The last stronghold of the die-hards, psychology, discovers only one human psyche, again infinite in its varieties. Man is one species.

Many scientists are cited in support of this vital truth in Professor Toynbee's monumental work A Study of History. The essence of the argument, after the biological proofs mentioned above, centres on the capacity for civilization in human beings and is summed up by Professor Dorsey in Why We Behave Like Human Beings:

There is no known fact of human anatomy or physiology which implies that capacity for culture or civilization or intelligence inheres in this race or that type . . . What wave did the Anglo-Saxon ride in the days of Tut-ankh-Amen, or of Caesar, or of William the Conqueror? How 'low' the savage European must have seemed to the Nile Valley African, looking north from his pyramid of Cheops![20]

We should also consider that there is only one way of

becoming a member of the human race; there are no preferential entrances or exits, whatever our ancestral history.

Bahá'u'lláh's simple metaphor 'the leaves of one tree' is the perfect statement. Every leaf on a tree is different; but every leaf is the same and readily recognizable as beech, oak or whatever.

The Oneness of Religion

Man did not create himself. Neither did he have any say in the conditions and circumstances of the universe which he inhabits, nor in the propensities of his own nature. With his intellect he has been able to discover something of the superb organization and laws of the physical universe, including his own body. But for all knowledge of spiritual things, the existence of one God, of his own soul, its powers and needs, the purpose of his life, he is dependent upon 'a succession of Great Souls especially appointed and empowered for the task, who are men and yet more than men . . . who inspire the onward movement of mankind and determine the manifold phases of human progress and enlightenment . . . For all that raises him above the level of a human animal man depends upon a new and special principle that is not found on the lower stages of being . . . and is the cause of all that is noble and gracious in life . . . [It] is the principle of God's Self-Manifestation in the human degree of existence.'[21]

One of the distinguishing features of Bahá'u'lláh's revelation is the illumination it sheds upon the nature of the Manifestation of God. Who is Christ? Who is Buddha? What is His reality, the source of His being, His power, knowledge and influence? The answer to these questions is the essential foundation for understanding the unity of religion, one of the sustaining pillars of world peace. For, as Bahá'u'lláh wrote, 'Religious fanaticism and hatred are a world-devouring fire, whose violence none can quench.'[22]

Bahá'u'lláh establishes first the utter transcendence of God:

To every discerning and illumined heart it is evident that God, the unknowable Essence, the divine Being, is immensely exalted beyond every human attribute, such as corporeal existence, ascent and descent, egress and regress. Far be it from His glory that human tongue should adequately recount His praise, or that human heart comprehend His fathomless mystery. He is and hath ever been veiled in the ancient eternity of His Essence, and will remain in His Reality everlastingly hidden from the sight of men. 'No vision taketh in Him, but He taketh in all vision; He is the Subtile, the All-Perceiving.' No tie of direct intercourse can possibly bind Him to His creatures. He standeth exalted beyond and above all separation and union, all proximity and remoteness. No sign can indicate His presence or His absence; inasmuch as by a word of His command all that are in heaven and on earth have come to exist, and by His wish, which is the Primal Will itself, all have stepped out of utter nothingness into the realm of being, the world of the visible.[23]

In one of the many hundreds of prayers which He revealed, we find the following:

All praise and glory be to Thee, Thou of Whom all things have testified that thou art one and there is none other God but Thee, Who hast been from everlasting exalted above all peer or likeness and to everlasting shalt remain the same. All kings are but Thy servants and all beings, visible and invisible, as naught before Thee. There is none other God but Thee, the Gracious, the Powerful, the Most High.[24]

And in almost every one of the prayers which He has given us, the last sentence in the above is repeated with variations on the names of God: the Almighty, the Pardoner, the Compassionate, the Help in peril, the Self-Subsisting.

But God has created us to know Him and to love Him, and therefore

. . . hath caused those luminous Gems of Holiness to appear out of the realm of the spirit, in the noble form of the human temple, and be made manifest unto all men, that they may impart unto the world the mysteries of the unchangeable Being, and tell of the subtleties of His imperishable Essence. These sanctified Mirrors, these Day-Springs of ancient glory are one and all the Exponents on earth of Him Who is the central Orb of the universe, its Essence and ultimate Purpose. From Him proceed their knowledge and power; from Him is derived their sovereignty. The beauty of their countenance is but a reflection of His image, and their revelation a sign of His deathless glory. They are the Treasuries of divine knowledge, and the Repositories of celestial wisdom. Through them is transmitted a grace that is infinite, and by them is revealed the light that can never fade. Even as He hath said: 'There is no distinction whatsoever between Thee and Them; except that they are Thy servants, and are created of Thee.'[25]

These are the Great Souls from whom we derive all our spiritual knowledge. Consider that there is no known record of a monotheistic society before Abraham. He was cast into fire and banished from His country for proclaiming it, but the Israelites accepted it and, in a world abounding with Egyptian, Persian, Assyrian, Greek, Roman and Arabian gods and goddesses, became known and sometimes ridiculed, sometimes feared for their one God. The commandments which Moses delivered at the behest of God have yet to be superseded and are indeed the foundation of all civilized life. On this basis of one God and law, Jesus, confirming the truth of eternal life, released into the world such a power of divine love as to set a new direction to men's ideals and hopes. The whole of Christendom has derived all its spiritual perceptions and noblest attainments from the influence of these three Manifestations of God. Muhammad, after breaking the idols, both physical and mental, of the barbarous tribes of Arabia, infused into them such a love of the one God and such a thirst for knowledge, that Islam became the most brilliant civilization the world had yet seen, and Baghdad became the centre of the world in arts and sciences. In the East it was Zoroaster and Buddha and Krishna who brought spiritual awareness, knowledge and perception to otherwise unenlightened generations of intellectuals bereft of divine guidance and open to all the illusions and imaginations of primitive men.

It is natural for man to worship God. If he has not been taught, he worships sticks and stones, a tree or mountain, or builds a totem pole to worship that, and he dreams of Valhalla, or happy hunting grounds or some other physical heaven. Until the Manifestation of God teaches him he knows nothing of the true reality of these aspirations within him. There is no other source of true knowledge of God, of ourselves, of the spiritual world. The eternal voice proclaims, 'Except ye enter through Me, no man entereth.'

This divine being has two natures. As man, sharing with us our human nature of physical body and rational soul, He comes into existence at a specific time. But His true and inward essence is eternal, coexistent with God, Who endows Him with His own power and knowledge. In this station He is of a higher order of being than man, and man has no access to that station. This eternal being is the spiritual Sun to man's spiritual nature. He is the Sun of Truth, the Word of God, by every one of which man lives. And like the physical sun, He appears at different times shining with a different intensity of light – morning, noon and evening, winter and summer, Monday, Tuesday and the rest – but in both worlds it is always the same Sun or sun. The spiritual Sun has the same effect on the hearts and souls and minds of men as the physical sun on the physical world. It melts the rigidity of the winter into which the old order has declined and promotes a new life in existent beings, bringing to consummation a new harvest of fruits and civilization.

In their human realities the Manifestations of God are different; in their spiritual reality they are one and the same Being, mirroring forth the Holy Spirit to the world of creation. Mankind has so far regarded them only in their distinction and differences, and the result has been 'different religions', enmity and virulent hatred between them – even between different sects of the same 'religion' – when all were created for the love of God. All the Manifestations of God have had the same purpose: the spiritual education of mankind in the love of God, the acquisition by man of spiritual virtues and the promotion of an ever-advancing civilization. Their spiritual teachings are the same; their counsels in mundane matters — diet, marriage, the organization of society — vary with conditions and circumstances.

Bahá'u'lláh devoted a great deal of His revelation to this all important subject. His *Kitáb-i-Íqán* or *Book of Certitude*, revealed in Baghdad in 1858 in the form of a letter to a relative of the Báb, is the main source of His teaching about it, while 'Abdu'l-Bahá in *Some Answered Questions* has a whole section of ten chapters 'On the Powers and Conditions of the Manifestations of God'. The following is a characteristic passage from the *Kitáb-i-Íqán*:

Furthermore, it is evident to thee that the Bearers of the trust of God are made manifest unto the peoples of the earth as the Exponents of a new Cause and the Bearers of a new Message. Inasmuch as these Birds of the Celestial Throne are all sent down from the heaven of the Will of God, and as they all arise to proclaim His irresistible Faith, they therefore are regarded as one soul and the same person. For they all drink from the one Cup of the love of God, and all partake of the fruit of the same Tree of Oneness. These Manifestations of God have each a twofold station. One is the station of pure abstraction and essential unity. In this respect, if thou callest them all by one name, and dost ascribe to them the same attribute, thou hast not erred from the truth . . . For they one and all summon the people of the earth to acknowledge the Unity of God, and herald unto them the Kawthar* of an infinite grace and bounty. They are all invested with the robe of Prophethood, and honoured with the mantle of glory . . . These Countenances are the recipients of the Divine Command, and the day-springs of His Revelation . . . It is clear and evident to thee that all the Prophets are the Temples of the Cause of God, Who have appeared clothed in divers attire. If thou wilt observe with discriminating eyes, thou

* A river in Paradise.

wilt behold them all abiding in the same tabernacle, soaring in the same heaven, seated upon the same throne, uttering the same speech, and proclaiming the same Faith. Such is the unity of those Essences of being, those Luminaries of infinite and immeasurable splendour.[26]

There are no false religions, only false prophets and false priests who arrogate power to themselves and corrupt, interpolate and pervert the meaning of the sacred text, adding to or detracting from it and devising rituals and ceremonies which eventually replace the divine message itself. Their leaders always reject and persecute the Manifestations of God as has been described.

The premises of one God and one human race lead inevitably to the conclusion of one religion, which is the relationship between God and man. There *is* only one religion, which is renewed from time to time as it suffers from the cooling of love, and as the changing circumstances of the world require and make possible further enlightenment. For the revelation is ever tempered to the needs and capacities of the stages of man's growth towards maturity. Jesus said that He could have revealed many things which we could not bear at that time, and Bahá'u'lláh states:

There can be no doubt whatever that the peoples of the world, of whatever race or religion, derive their inspiration from one heavenly Source, and are the subjects of one God. The difference between the ordinances under which they abide should be attributed to the varying requirements and exigencies of the age in which they were revealed.[27]

Consort with the followers of all religions in a spirit of friendliness and fellowship.[28]

The Bahá'í therefore, knowing that all men, including the atheist and doubter, are the creation of one God, that he is the brother of every man and woman on earth, armed with the power of God manifest anew in this Day of God, can make the greatest and surest contribution to the peace of the world that is possible. Greeting his co-religionist from any communion, he may share the delights of a large field of mutual agreement, discuss without rancour and with interest points of difference, and remembering how Bahá'u'lláh dealt with the young dervish who was 'cooking God',* may offer the adamant fundamentalist another view of talking snakes and magic apples and stars falling on the earth and bodies going up and coming down on clouds.

Religion has always given man the most satisfying picture of the universe, at each stage of his development. As J. B. Priestley pointed out,[29] the description of the earth as a green platform suspended between heaven above and hell below, on which God and the Devil fought for the souls of men, was intensely satisfying to medieval man and provided a firm base for a general civilization – in this instance Christendom. While the battle for the life of man's soul is ever with us, the geography of that simple picture could not survive the discoveries of science; and religion, whose obscurantist leaders sought to hold back the tide of knowledge, increasingly lost its hold on the minds of men.

Without some such general philosophy it is not possible to develop a unified society. When religion fails, human affairs decline into chaos, as our own days testify. If the answer to 'why' is only futility, then the world becomes a cockpit for the ultimate pursuit of every human passion and vice, and without any sanction on his conduct, man becomes lower than the animal. World peace is impossible in such conditions.

The universe which Bahá'u'lláh discloses to our minds is at once satisfying, uplifting, wonderful and glorious. It discloses the sovereignty of God and His purpose in creating man. It makes science and religion equal partners in every man's philosophy. To science is allotted, through man's intellect, the discovery of 'what' and 'how'; religion provides the answers

* See page 44.

to 'why' and 'for what purpose', and prescribes the parameters of human conduct and the mores of God's Kingdom on this earth. Bahá'u'lláh proclaims:

All men have been created to carry forward an ever-advancing civilization.[30]

and

The Purpose of the one true God, exalted be His glory, in revealing Himself unto men is to lay bare those gems that lie hidden within the mine of their true and inmost selves.[31]

These are objective aims which are continuously pursued and continually attained in degrees as mankind grows up. There is no final attainment to either as both goals and both processes are infinite.

Over all and beyond every other consideration is the eternal mystery of 'why' which takes us into the subjective worlds of mysticism and spiritual perception, to the point beyond which there is no passing. This is the realm of divine love, which once tasted none other will suffice. It is the Holy Spirit of God and is the active agent in all creation. All can review its bounties; none can understand it. It is radiated from the Manifestation of God and produces its effect in the world. It is the sustaining force of all existence and were it to falter for less than the twinkling of an eye, the entire creation would cease to exist.

Bahá'u'lláh, walking the banks of the Tigris, composed a series of verses in Persian and Arabic known as *Hidden Words*. They are gems of divine comment upon the love of God for man, why God created him, how close to him – closer than his life's vein – He is, and yet how man remains far from God and entertains other love in his heart.

O SON OF MAN!
Veiled in My immemorial being and in the ancient eternity of My essence, I knew My love for thee; therefore I created thee, have engraved on thee Mine image and revealed to thee My beauty.

O SON OF MAN!

I loved thy creation, hence I created thee. Wherefore, do thou love Me, that I may name thy name and fill thy soul with the spirit of life.

O SON OF BEING!

Love Me, that I may love thee. If thou lovest Me not, My love can in no wise reach thee. Know this, O servant.

O SON OF SPIRIT!

There is no peace for thee save by renouncing thyself and turning unto Me; for it behoveth thee to glory in My name, not in thine own; to put thy trust in Me and not in thyself, since I desire to be loved alone and above all that is.

O SON OF SPIRIT!

I created thee rich, why dost thou bring thyself down to poverty? Noble I made thee, wherewith dost thou abase thyself? Out of the essence of knowledge I gave thee being, why seekest thou enlightenment from anyone beside Me?

O SON OF UTTERANCE!

Turn thy face unto Mine and renounce all save Me; for My sovereignty endureth and My dominion perisheth not. If thou seekest another than Me, yea, if thou searchest the universe for evermore, thy quest will be in vain.

O SON OF THE SUPREME!

I have made death a messenger of joy to thee. Wherefore dost thou grieve? I made the light to shed on thee its splendour. Why dost thou veil thyself therefrom?

O SON OF WORLDLINESS!

Pleasant is the realm of being, wert thou to attain thereto; glorious is the domain of eternity, shouldst thou pass beyond the world of mortality; sweet is the holy ecstasy if thou drinkest of the mystic chalice from the hands of the celestial Youth. Shouldst thou attain this station, thou wouldst be freed from destruction and death, from toil and sin.[32]

. . . . .

Shoghi Effendi in one of his expository essays, *The Unfold-*

ment of World Civilization, has penned this vision of the coming Kingdom:

Unification of the whole of mankind is the hall-mark of the stage which human society is now approaching. Unity of the family, of tribe, of city-state, and nation have been successively attempted and fully established. World unity is the goal towards which a harassed humanity is striving. Nation-building has come to an end. The anarchy inherent in state sovereignty is moving towards a climax. A world, growing to maturity, must abandon this fetish, recognize the oneness and wholeness of human relationships, and establish once for all the machinery that can best incarnate this fundamental principle of its life.

'A new life', Bahá'u'lláh proclaims, 'is, in this age, stirring within all the peoples of the earth; and yet none hath discovered its cause, or perceived its motive.' 'O ye children of men,' He thus addresses His generation, 'the fundamental purpose animating the Faith of God and His Religion is to safeguard the interests and promote the unity of the human race . . . This is the straight path, the fixed and immovable foundation. Whatsoever is raised on this foundation, the changes and chances of the world can never impair its strength, nor will the revolution of countless centuries undermine its structure.'

. . . The unity of the human race, as envisaged by Bahá'u'lláh, implies the establishment of a world commonwealth in which all nations, races, creeds and classes are closely and permanently united, and in which the autonomy of its state members and the personal freedom and initiative of the individuals that compose them are definitely and completely safeguarded. This commonwealth must, as far as we can visualize it, consist of a world legislature, whose members will, as the trustees of the whole of mankind, ultimately control the entire resources of all the component nations, and will enact such laws as shall be required to regulate the life, satisfy the needs and adjust the relationships of all races and peoples. A world executive, backed by an international Force, will carry out the decisions arrived at, and apply the laws enacted by, this world legislature, and will safeguard the organic unity of the whole commonwealth. A world tribunal will adjudicate and deliver its compulsory and final verdict in all and any disputes that may arise between the various elements constituting this universal system. A mechanism of world inter-communication will be devised, embracing the whole planet, freed from national hindrances and restrictions, and functioning with marvellous swiftness and perfect regularity. A world metropolis will act as the nerve centre of a world civilization, the focus towards which the unifying forces of life will converge and from which its energizing influences will radiate. A world language will either be invented or chosen from among the existing languages and will be taught in the schools of all the federated nations as an auxiliary to their mother tongue. A world script, a world literature, a uniform and universal system of currency, of weights and measures, will simplify and facilitate intercourse and understanding among the nations and races of mankind. In such a world society, science and religion, the two most potent forces in human life will be reconciled, will cooperate, and will harmoniously develop. The press will, under such a system, while giving full scope to the expression of the diversified views and convictions of mankind, cease to be mischievously manipulated by vested interests, whether private or public, and will be liberated from the influence of contending governments and peoples. The economic resources of the world will be organized, its sources of raw materials will be tapped and fully utilized, its markets will be coordinated and developed, and the distribution of its products will be equitably regulated.

National rivalries, hatreds, and intrigues will cease, and racial animosity and prejudice will be replaced by racial amity, under-standing and cooperation. The causes of religious strife will be permanently removed, economic barriers and restrictions will be completely abolished, and the inordinate distinction between classes will be obliterated. Destitution on the one hand, and gross accumulation of ownership on the other, will disappear. The enormous energy dissipated and wasted on war, whether economic or political, will be consecrated to such ends as will extend the range of human inventions and technical development, to the increase of the productivity of mankind, to the extermination of disease, to the extension of scientific research, to the raising of the standard of physical health, to the sharpening and refinement of the human brain, to the exploitation of the unused and unsuspected resources of the planet, to the prolongation of human life, and to the furtherance of any other agency that can stimulate the intellectual, the moral, and spiritual life of the entire human race.

A world federal system, ruling the whole earth and exercising unchallengeable authority over its unimaginably vast resources, blending and embodying the ideals of both the East and the West, liberated from the curse of war and its miseries, and bent on the exploitation of all the available sources of energy on the surface of the planet, a system in which Force is made the servant of Justice, whose life is sustained by its universal recognition of one God and by its allegiance to one common Revelation – such is the goal towards which humanity, impelled by the unifying forces of life, is moving.[33]

The Most Great Peace is a new civilization, a new world order, not imposed from the top as an ideology, but springing from firmly-held grass roots conviction of the oneness of mankind and the fundamental oneness of religion. Viewed from this basis the earth is indeed but one country and mankind its citizens. On this foundation of oneness men may see their differences as a gardener sees the variety of his plants or a conductor the various instruments in his orchestra; all are valuable and all make their contribution to the perfect outcome.

A world civilization requires a world 'mythology'. Day by day Bahá'u'lláh becomes more widely recognized as that supernal figure – the Manifestation of God – who, at certain moments in history has appeared in different places and under different names to become the mystical centre from which have radiated the spiritual sinews and ethics of great civilizations and to which have returned the prayers and adoration of faithful millions. Knowledge of the new revelation is penetrating human consciousness, reviving man's failing spirit, restoring his love of God and setting the bird of his heart in a new direction towards the realization of that glorious apocalyptic vision unveiled in the sacred books of the past and bedded deep in mankind's aspiration.

Chapter 4

THE NEW REVELATION

THE Middle East at the end of the eighteenth century not only shared in the general world decline, but was the very epitome of a dark age, relapsed from a great civilization. The brilliance of Islam, which in its heyday had illumined the world, was gone, and ignorance, fanaticism, dirt and disease were prevalent throughout the Muslim world. Iran was at the nadir of this condition. But it was from the horizon of that dark and abysmal country that mankind's day of deliverance dawned.

The new revelation was attended by all the signs and portents associated with the birth of a world religion. Its Herald – the Báb – was a Prophet in His own right, announced by forerunners who prepared the way for His coming. In Shiraz He made His declaration to His first disciple one day before, on the other side of the world, that first telegram was sent. From Baltimore to Washington the wires carried the message, 'What hath God wrought'.

The Báb occupies an unique position in mankind's religious history. He was not only the Promised One of Islam but emphatically and repeatedly announced the imminent appearance of that One who would fulfil the expectations of all the world religions. He, the Báb, was the Herald of that Promised One of all ages, the Lord of Hosts, the Prince of Peace, who would inaugurate the long-awaited, Christ-promised Kingdom of God on earth, and reveal the laws and ordinances, the spiritual and social principles which would establish and vitalize the coming era of human felicity. The Báb referred to Him as 'He whom God shall make manifest'.

The Báb's claim and announcement aroused immediately the fierce opposition of the Muslim clergy. Their reaction was the same as had been that of the Pharisees to the message of Jesus, and they conspired with the same fanatical hatred to destroy the Báb and His followers. Iran's sleep of death was shattered and a period of incredible turmoil ensued. During those first persecutions thousands of men, women and children were martyred in circumstances of horrible cruelty. In 1850 the Báb Himself was publicly executed in Tabriz.

The short but turbulent history of the Báb is recorded in the reports and letters of European diplomats and representatives to the court of the Shah as well as in the immortal narrative of Nabíl,[1] a Bábí who survived the holocaust. It engaged the interest of intellectual Europe and became a leading subject in their discussions.[2]

However, it was not the Báb's teachings, nor His announcement of the imminent appearance of the Promised One of all ages, but rather His own youthful charm and tragic martyrdom and the savagery with which His followers were exterminated which attracted the attention of the European world. They did not discern that His brief dispensation was the turning point in humanity's spiritual history, His revelation the link, the period of transition between the old, prophetic, growing-up age of mankind, and the new era of maturity. Arising in the east, it was the spiritual dawn of the new Day of God.

The Báb had assigned to each of His disciples — the Letters of the Living, as they were called — a specific task and sent them throughout the country to prepare the people for the coming of 'He Whom God shall make manifest'. His address to them, a few days after His declaration, left them in no doubt that a new dispensation in the eternal religion of God had opened. The following is a shortened version of that address:

O My beloved friends! You are the bearers of the name of God in this Day. You have been chosen as the repositories of His mystery. It behoves each one of you to manifest the attributes of God, and to exemplify by your deeds and words the signs of His righteousness, His power and glory. The very members of your body must bear witness to the loftiness of your purpose, the integrity of your life, the reality of your faith, and the exalted character of your devotion. For verily I say, this is the Day spoken of by God in His Book . . . Ponder the words of Jesus addressed to His disciples, as He sent them forth to propagate the Cause of God. In words such as these, He bade them arise and fulfil their mission: 'Ye are even as the fire which in the darkness of the night has been kindled upon the mountain-top. Let your light shine before the eyes of men . . . You are the salt of the earth, but if the salt have lost its savour, wherewith shall it be salted? Such must be the degree of your detachment, that into whatever city you enter to proclaim and teach the Cause of God, you should in no wise expect either meat or reward from its people. Nay, when you depart out of that city, you should shake the dust from off your feet . . .' O My Letters! Verily I say, immensely exalted is this Day above the days of the Apostles of old. Nay, immeasurable is the difference! You are the witnesses of the Dawn of the promised Day of God . . . Scatter throughout the length and breadth of this land, and, with steadfast feet and sanctified hearts, prepare the way for His coming. Heed not your weakness and frailty; fix your gaze upon the invincible power your the Lord, your God, the Almighty. Has He not, in past days, caused Abraham, in spite of His seeming helplessness, to triumph over the forces of Nimrod? Has He not enabled Moses, whose staff was His only companion, to vanquish Pharaoh and his hosts? Has He not established the ascendancy of Jesus, poor and lowly as He was in the eyes of men, over the combined forces of the Jewish people? Has He not subjected the barbarous and militant tribes of Arabia to the holy and transforming discipline of Muḥammad, His Prophet? Arise in His name, put your trust wholly in Him, and be assured of ultimate victory.

To Mullá Ḥusayn, the first to believe in Him, He entrusted a special mission. He directed him to Teheran, a 'city which enshrines a Mystery of such transcendent holiness as neither

Ḥijáz* nor S͟híráz† can hope to rival'.[3] Mullá Ḥusayn was to deliver a letter from the Báb to an exalted person in that city to whom he would be guided.

* Refers to Muhammad.
† Refers to the Báb.

Chapter 5

THE NOBLEMAN OF NÚR

BAHÁ'U'LLÁH was born to the purple, and the first twenty-seven years of His life were spent in ducal affluence, enjoying all the advantages conferred by noble birth and riches. He was born in Teheran on November 12th, 1817 and was known as Mírzá Ḥusayn-'Alí. He grew up among the courtiers of the Shah, moving as the season dictated between the family's palatial country estate and the mansion in the capital.

He derived His descent, on the one hand, from Abraham (the Father of the Faithful) through his wife Katurah, and on the other from Zoroaster, as well as from Yazdigird, the last king of the Sásáníyán dynasty. He was moreover a descendant of Jesse,* and belonged, through His father, Mirzá 'Abbás, better known as Mírzá Buzurg – a nobleman closely associated with the ministerial circles of the Court of Fath-'Alí Sháh – to one of the most ancient and renowned families of Mázindarán.[1]

The Persian nobility of those days were not among the world's thinkers, scientists, and philosophers. Generally they had little education beyond a superficial knowledge of the sacred scriptures of Islam and the better known works of Persian literature; they were taught to ride, handle a gun and wield a sword. They excelled in the art of calligraphy. Persia itself was in abysmal decay. It was, in Lord Curzon's phrase,

---

* This is not Jesse the father of David, but the Jesse referred to in Isaiah 11:1,10.

'a church state' where the whole way of life was subject to the interpretation of Islam given by a horde of ignorant clergy, who, in spite of the command of the Qur'án to seek for knowledge, condemned science as western devilry. There were no courts of law or constitutional rights. Mírzá Buzurg's family came from Núr, the district of Mázindarán on the borders of the Caspian Sea where their estates were situated. They were renowned for their wealth and responsible use of it, a trait which distinguished them from the majority of their peers.

From the earliest days of His life Bahá'u'lláh was recognized as one apart. Precocious and remarkably talented children are not unusual, but Bahá'u'lláh's distinction lay beyond those characteristics. There was an exaltation about Him, a natural grandeur which, allied to a modesty and geniality, made Him, even in childhood, the object of widespread admiration and love. He learned to read and write but did not pursue any scholarly or academic studies. Yet He freely engaged in discussions of subjects normally considered the preserves of theologians and scholars, and astounded the religious doctors and the learned by His knowledge, His clear reasoning and irrefutable logic. At the age of seven He presented a case on behalf of His father before the Shah, and whether by His childish appeal or the cogency of His argument, won the monarch's approval.

His mother expressed astonishment that He neither cried nor became restless and His father quickly realized that he had an extraordinary son, whom he came to love ever more deeply. One night in a dream he saw Bahá'u'lláh swimming in a vast, limitless ocean:

His body shone upon the water with a radiance that illumined the sea. Around His head, which could distinctly be seen above the waters, there radiated, in all directions, His long, jet-black locks, floating in great profusion above the waves. As he dreamed, a multitude of fishes gathered round Him, each holding fast to the extremity of one hair. Fascinated by the effulgences of His face, they followed Him in whatever direction He swam. Great as was their number, and however firmly they clung to His locks, not one single hair seemed to have been detached from His head, nor did the least injury affect His person. Free and unrestrained, He moved above the waters and they all followed Him.

Nabíl records that Bahá'u'lláh's father, the vizier, summoned a renowned mystic of the region and asked him to interpret the dream.

This man, as if inspired by a premonition of the future glory of Bahá'u'lláh, declared: 'The limitless ocean that you have seen in your dream, O Vazír, is none other than the world of being. Single-handed and alone, your son will achieve supreme ascendancy over it. Wherever He may please, He will proceed unhindered. No one will resist His march, no one will hinder His progress. The multitude of fishes signifies the turmoil which He will arouse amidst the peoples and kindreds of the earth. Around Him will they gather, and to Him will they cling. Assured of the unfailing protection of the Almighty, this tumult will never harm His person, nor will His loneliness upon the sea of life endanger His safety.'[2]

Dr J. E. Esslemont, one of the first British Bahá'ís, recorded that 'Abdu'l-Bahá one day related to him the following about Bahá'u'lláh:

From childhood He was extremely kind and generous. He was a great lover of outdoor life, most of His time being spent in the garden or the fields. He had an extraordinary power of attraction, which was felt by all. People always crowded around Him, Ministers and people of the Court would surround Him, and the children also were devoted to Him. When He was only thirteen or fourteen years old He became renowned for His learning. He would converse on any subject and solve any problem presented to Him. In large gatherings He would discuss matters with the 'Ulamá (leading mullás) and would explain intricate religious questions. All of them used to listen to Him with the greatest interest.

When Bahá'u'lláh was twenty-two years old, His father died, and the Government wished Him to succeed to His father's position in the Ministry, as was customary in Persia, but Bahá'u'lláh did not accept the offer. Then the Prime Minister said: 'Leave him to himself. Such a position is unworthy of him. He has some higher aim in view. I cannot understand him, but I am convinced that he is destined for some lofty career. His thoughts are not like ours. Let him alone.'[3]

A charming incident is related of one of those days when Bahá'u'lláh, with a few companions, was riding in the country-side. Espying a young man, alone by a brook, near which he had kindled a fire and was cooking and eating his food, Bahá'u'lláh enquired in friendly manner, 'What are you doing, dervish?' 'I am cooking and eating God,' was the answer. Bahá'u'lláh was so interested by the simplicity of this reply and the youth's unaffected manner that He alighted and engaged him in conversation. The friendly affection displayed by Bahá'u'lláh quickly won the heart of that youth, who in a short time accepted the more enlightened view of God which Bahá'u'lláh offered to him and became so enamoured of this genial, mysterious stranger that he abandoned his cooking utensils and followed Him. On foot, behind His horse, he danced along singing the verses of a love song which he composed as he went. 'Thou art the Day-Star of guidance; Thou art the light of Truth,' he chanted. 'Unveil Thyself' was his constant refrain. His name was Muṣṭafá and his poem later had a wide circulation among the dervishes of that area. Nabíl, who relates this episode, wondered whether the unlettered dervish, uplifted to so joyful a condition, had been allowed to catch a glimpse of that supernal glory which as yet was concealed from the eyes of men.[4]

Bahá'u'lláh had an overwhelming passion for justice. He championed the cause of the poor and the oppressed, and none who turned to him for help was refused. He withdrew from the life of the court and even as a young man became known as 'the Father of the poor'. In 1835, when He was nearly eighteen, He married 'Ásíyih Khánum, whom He entitled Navváb,* from the nearby town of Yálrúd. She was the daughter of a vizier of comparable wealth to Mírzá Buzurg's, causing people to comment, 'It is adding wealth to wealth.' (Navváb's wedding treasures were carried on the backs of forty mules). But it was also said of Bahá'u'lláh that even His vast wealth could not survive the liberality which He extended. It was His love for humanity, His moral eminence and the respect accorded Him by courtier and peasant alike which convinced Mullá Husayn, on his arrival in Teheran, that Mírzá Husayn-'Alí — Bahá'u'lláh — was the exalted person to whom he must deliver the letter from the Báb.

The story of how Mullá Husayn was led to Bahá'u'lláh is of great interest and pertinence to our theme. Arrived in Teheran he settled himself in a room of a religious college and approached the eminent divine who was head of that college. To him he conveyed the news of the dawning revelation, only to be severely reprimanded. The conversation was overheard and deeply deplored by one of the students at that college, who felt himself greatly drawn to Mullá Husayn and attracted by his message. So affected was he by all that he had heard that at midnight, in a state of great perturbation, he knocked on the door of Mullá Husayn's room and unburdened his heart to him. Mullá Husayn recognized in this unusual visit the guidance he was seeking, and the following conversation, paraphrased from Nabil's account, ensued.[5]

'I can now see why I chose to dwell in this place. What is your name and where do you live?'

'My name is Mullá Muhammad and I come from Núr in the province of Mázindarán.'

'Is there today, among the family of the late Mírzá Buzurg-

---

* Navváb was Bahá'u'lláh's first wife, the mother of 'Abdu'l-Bahá, Bahíyyih Khánum and Mírzá Mihdí. In 1849, a younger brother died and Bahá'u'lláh, in accordance with approved custom and expectation, married the widow. Later, in Baghdad, the widow of a martyr fled to Him for protection, which He afforded her in the only way possible, by taking her as His third wife. These marriages were within the Muslim law and custom and took place before the Declaration of Bahá'u'lláh's mission and the revelation of His book of laws, the *Kitáb-i-Aqdas*, which prescribes monogamy.

i-Núrí, anyone capable of maintaining the high character and traditions of that illustrious house?'

'Yes. One of his sons has proved himself, by his virtuous life, his high attainments, his loving-kindness and liberality, a noble descendant of a noble father.'

'What is his occupation?'

'He cheers the disconsolate and feeds the hungry.'

'What of his rank and position?'

'He has none, apart from befriending the poor and the stranger.'

'What is his name?'

'Husayn-'Alí.'

'How does he spend his time?'

'He roams the woods and delights in the beauties of the countryside.'

'What is his age?'

'Eight and twenty.'

'I presume you often meet him?'

'I frequently visit his house.'

'Will you deliver into his hands a trust from me?'

'Most assuredly.'

Mullá Ḥusayn then gave him the Báb's letter, wrapped in a piece of cloth as was the Persian custom, with the earnest request that he deliver it the next day and be kind enough to inform him of the reply. Mullá Muḥammad went early next morning to Bahá'u'lláh's house in Teheran where he found Mírzá Músá, Bahá'u'lláh's brother, standing at the gate. Mírzá Músá ushered him into Bahá'u'lláh's presence and laid the letter before him.

Nabíl records that Bahá'u'lláh scanned the letter and then began to read certain of its passages aloud. At the end of a page He stopped and, turning to Mírzá Músá, declared it to be endowed with the same regenerating power as the Qur'án.

This moment was a critical turning point in Bahá'u'lláh's life. The great nobleman, possessed of vast wealth, power and influence, *persona grata* at the Court, was presented with a claim which He recognized instantly to be the long-awaited religious reformation so desperately needed in His country, and which, He well knew, would bring down upon all who supported it the hatred and bitter persecution of the ruling classes of the realm — the corrupted clergy and the degenerate officialdom.

Not for one moment did He hesitate. He sent the young student back to Mullá Ḥusayn with a gift and arose to proclaim the new message, thereby embracing for Himself whatever would come in the path of God, from which He never wavered or retreated. Despoliation, torture, imprisonment, exile, calumniation and hatred, whatever the human race could heap upon Him were powerless to stay the accomplishment of His mission, which He proclaimed from prison and banishment to the kings and rulers and peoples of the world. He would, at the command of God and with His power, regenerate and unify mankind and lay the foundation of peace on earth.

Chapter 6

MÍRZÁ ḤUSAYN-'ALÍ, THE BÁBÍ

THE first journey which Bahá'u'lláh undertook to promote the new revelation was to His ancestral home in Núr. His unaccountable knowledge, His brilliant eloquence and high attainments were already a byword in that part of Iran and He was welcomed home with great enthusiasm. Large numbers of the officials and people of eminence called on Him, eager to learn the news of the capital and the court. But Bahá'u'lláh disdained such gossip and eloquently presented the message of the new revelation, emphasizing the benefits it would bring to their country.

Many of those who heard Him were so deeply impressed that they themselves set out to tell others. Tidings of the new message spread rapidly throughout Mázindarán and other provinces of Iran, winning supporters not only from among the great mass of the downtrodden and oppressed but in large measure from among the literate, the younger divines and the higher ranks of the social order. Lord Curzon in his *Persia and the Persian Question* declared that its recruits were gained from among the nobler minds of Islam.

Bahá'u'lláh lent the full weight of His influence and wealth to its support. He made a journey into Iraq to the holy city of Karbila to encourage the Bábís there. Returned to Iran, His was the guiding genius of the critical Conference of Badasht where Bábís from various provinces gathered as His guests to discuss their situation. Many dramatic events took place, not the least being the sudden appearance, unveiled, of Ṭáhirih, the famed poetess and champion of women's emancipation. It was here that the independence of the new Faith was openly proclaimed and the transition from the ecclesiasticism, traditions and ceremonials of the past made clear.

Bahá'u'lláh's high position, wealth and influence enabled Him for a short time to render immense services to the new Faith, but eventually He too was engulfed in the fierce wave of fanatical hatred which the clergy of Shi'ah Islam unleashed against it. 'Governors, magistrates and civil servants, throughout the provinces, instigated by the monstrous campaign of vilification conducted by the clergy, and prompted by their lust for pecuniary rewards, vied in their respective spheres with each other in hounding and heaping indignities on the adherents of an outlawed Faith.'[1] Insulted by a mob which pelted Him with stones, twice imprisoned by local officials, bastinadoed until His feet bled, Bahá'u'lláh was eventually ordered by Muḥammad Sháh himself, giving in to persistent misrepresentations, to be arrested and brought to the capital. This order was never carried out due to the sudden death of the sovereign.

But this was no more than a temporary reprieve. The all-powerful 'ulamá,* having done to death the Báb, and having eliminated the great figures who had so heroically illumined the tragic history of His brief dispensation, now recognized Bahá'u'lláh as the one remaining obstacle to their declared intention of eradicating this hated heresy from the soil of Iran. Bahá'u'lláh became the focal point of their hatred and His destruction their goal.

The opportunity they wanted presented itself. An attempt was made on the life of the Shah by an obscure Bábí youth, an assistant in a confectioner's shop, who, driven to despair by the martyrdom of his beloved Master, loaded a pistol with bird-shot incapable of killing a man. With two equally

* religious leaders

youthful companions, he waited at the roadside outside the monarch's summer palace. As the Shah emerged, on horseback, the youth discharged his pistol at him and some of its pellets found their mark, lightly wounding him.

The outcry was at once raised that here was evidence of a Bábí plot to overthrow the monarchy and subvert the government. The young Bábí was immediately disposed of and the pieces of his body exhibited about Teheran. His companions were tortured and similarly dispatched. In a short time every known Bábí and anyone who, for whatever reason, could be designated as such, were at peril of life. The savagery of the holocaust which followed roused the indignation and horror of Europe, whose intellectuals and savants, as already noted, made the Báb a subject of prime interest.

Bahá'u'lláh, at the time of the incident, was the guest of the Grand Vizier in a village near the Shah's summer residence, where the imperial army was encamped. Refusing the advice of His friends, Bahá'u'lláh rode out boldly towards the imperial camp, much to the astonishment of His enemies, who had set out to arrest Him. He was apprehended, despite the intervention of the Russian Minister, Prince Dolgorouki, and hurried along the road to the horrendous Síyáh-Chál, the Black Pit of Teheran, 'a place foul beyond comparison'. He declared His complete innocence of 'that evil deed', a fact which was established by several tribunals. He recalled being conducted 'on foot and in chains, with bared head and bare feet, to the dungeon of Tihrán'.[2]

The ubiquitous mob lined the roadside to jeer and throw their refuse at Him, Who had ever been their friend and benefactor. Among them was an old woman with a stone in her hand, unable to keep pace with the procession. 'Give me a chance to fling my stone in his face', she pleaded. Bahá'u'lláh urged the guard not to deny her what she regarded as a meritorious act in the sight of God.

Some seventy years later, Bahá'u'lláh's eldest daughter, Bahíyyih Khánum, in the evening of her life, related to Lady

Blomfield, one of the first English Bahá'ís, her memories of
the tragic events of those days. They are recorded in *The Chosen
Highway*, from which this extract is taken:

From our doors nobody was ever turned away; the hospitable board
was spread for all comers . . .

Whilst the people called my father 'The Father of the Poor', they
spoke of my mother as 'The Mother of Consolation', though,
naturally, only the women and little children ever looked upon her
face unveiled . . .

One day I remember very well, though I was only six years old
at the time. It seemed that an attempt had been made on the life
of the Sháh by a half-crazy young Bábí.

My father was away at his country house in the village of
Niyávarán, which was his property, the villagers of which were all
and individually cared for by him.

Suddenly and hurriedly a servant came rushing in great distress
to my mother.

'The master, the master, he is arrested – I have seen him! He has
walked many miles! Oh, they have beaten him. They say he has
suffered the torture of the bastinado! His feet are bleeding! He has
no shoes on! His turban has gone! His clothes are torn! There are
chains upon his neck!'

My poor mother's face grew whiter and whiter.

We children were terribly frightened and could only weep
bitterly.

Immediately everybody, all our relations, and friends, and
servants fled from our house in terror, only one man-servant,
Isfandíyár, remained, and one woman. Our palace, and the smaller
houses belonging to it were very soon stripped of everything;
furniture, treasures, all were stolen by the people.[3]

Bahá'u'lláh's brother, Mírzá Músá, who remained faithful
throughout his life, helped the distraught mother and her
three children to escape and found them a small house near
the prison where they could remain in hiding. Ásíyih Khánum
gathered what small treasures she could, such as the gold
buttons on her wedding dress, and sold everything to provide
money to pay the gaolers to take food to Bahá'u'lláh and to

keep the family alive. Navváb, as Ásíyih <u>Kh</u>ánum was known, features heroically throughout this episode and the remaining years of tragedy and exile. She died in 'Akká in 1886 and her remains now lie beside those of her illustrious daughter and younger son, surmounted by befitting monuments in the Bahá'í gardens on Mount Carmel.

The pogrom against the Bábís was now let loose, and all hopes, fears, rumours and prayers were focused on Bahá'u'lláh. Would He be destroyed? None knew the outcome.

Chapter 7

PRISONER IN THE
SÍYÁH-CHÁL

THE infamous Síyáh-Chál — the Black Pit of Teheran — was an underground dungeon to which no ray of sunlight ever penetrated. It had once been the reservoir of a public bath. Few survived its rigours for long.

Immediately on receipt of the news of the attempted assassination of the Shah, the authorities in Teheran herded together some eighty known Bábís and upon the arrival of Bahá'u'lláh in the circumstances already related, chained Him and them together and cast them into this black hole. Bahá'u'lláh Himself relates:

Upon our arrival We were first conducted along a pitch-black corridor, from whence We descended three steep flights of stairs to the place of confinement assigned to Us. The dungeon was wrapped in thick darkness, and Our fellow-prisoners numbered nearly a hundred and fifty souls: thieves, assassins and highwaymen. Though crowded, it had no other outlet than the passage by which We entered. No pen can depict that place, nor any tongue describe its loathsome smell. Most of these men had neither clothes nor bedding to lie on. God alone knoweth what befell Us in that most foul-smelling and gloomy place![1]

This prison prized highly and was famous for two of its chief instruments, the dreaded chains known as Salásil and Qará-Guhar. Bahá'u'lláh declared that for four months He was 'tormented and chained by one or the other of them'.[2]

The prisoners were placed in two rows, facing each other over the stocks in which their feet were held. The air they breathed was foul; the stone floor was covered with filth and infested with vermin and no warmth relieved the dungeon's icy gloom. Every day one of them was released from his stocks and chains and taken to the gallows. Bahá'u'lláh related how He taught the facing lines to sing verses in response to each other. One row would sing, 'God is sufficient unto me; He verily is the All-Sufficing!', and the other would reply, 'In Him let the trusting trust.'[3]

'Abdu'l-Bahá, eight years old, went to see His father in the prison. He related that half-way down the steps to the cell it became so dark that He could not see anything. He heard Bahá'u'lláh call out, 'Take him away.' He was taken out and seated to wait for the prisoners to be brought out for their meal.

I saw Bahá'u'lláh's neck in chains, and another, both chained to the same links, a link about His neck and another about the person who was chained with Him. The weight of the chain was so excessive that His neck was bent; He walked with great difficulty, and He was in a very sad condition. His clothes were tattered and battered; even the hat on His head was torn. He was in the most severe ordeal and His health was quite visibly failing. They brought me and seated me, and they took Him to the place where there was a pond, in order that He might wash His face. After that they took Him back to the dungeon and, although I was a child, I was so overcome I was unconscious.[4]

It was in these dark and dismal surroundings, amid such appalling conditions that 'He whom God shall make manifest', Christ returned in the glory of the Father, received His divine mandate and was invested with the powers and authority of the Promised One of all ages, the Prince of Peace, anticipated, longed for, prayed for in all the revealed religions of mankind.

Comparable only to the episodes of Moses and the Burning Bush, Zoroaster and the Seven Visions, Buddha under the

Bodhi tree, the descent of the Dove upon Jesus, the voice of Gabriel commanding Muhammad to *'cry in the name of thy Lord'*, Bahá'u'lláh's experience in the Síyáh-Chál is unique:

During the days I lay in the prison in Ṭihrán, though the galling weight of the chains and the stench-filled air allowed Me but little sleep, still in those infrequent moments of slumber I felt as if something flowed from the crown of My head over My breast, even as a mighty torrent that precipitateth itself upon the earth from the summit of a lofty mountain. Every limb of My body would, as a result, be set afire. At such moments My tongue recited what no man could bear to hear.[5]

One night, in a dream, these exalted words were heard on every side: 'Verily, We shall render Thee victorious by Thyself and by Thy Pen. Grieve Thou not for that which hath befallen Thee, neither be Thou afraid, for Thou art in safety. Erelong will God raise up the treasures of the earth – men who will aid Thee through Thyself and through Thy Name, wherewith God hath revived the hearts of such as have recognized Him.'[6]

While engulfed in tribulations I heard a most wondrous, a most sweet voice, calling above My head. Turning My face, I beheld a Maiden – the embodiment of the remembrance of the name of My Lord – suspended in the air before Me. So rejoiced was she in her very soul that her countenance shone with the ornament of the good-pleasure of God, and her cheeks glowed with the brightness of the All-Merciful. Betwixt earth and heaven she was raising a call which captivated the hearts and minds of men. She was imparting to both My inward and outer being tidings which rejoiced My soul, and the souls of God's honoured servants. Pointing with her finger unto My head, she addressed all who are in heaven and all who are on earth, saying: 'By God! this is the Best-Beloved of the worlds, and yet ye comprehend not. This is the Beauty of God amongst you, and the power of His sovereignty within you, could ye but understand. This is the Mystery of God and His Treasure, the Cause of God and His glory unto all who are in the kingdoms of Revelation and of creation, if ye be of them that perceive.'[7]

In the entire religious history of mankind there has been no such direct, clear and circumstantial account of the investiture by God in His chosen revealer of the majesty, power and authority which is always His. This is the Spirit, the Being, Who was before Abraham and eternally shall be.

Chapter 8

EXILE

NONE knew of Bahá'u'lláh's apotheosis in that dank and dismal place, an experience which rendered Him immune to whatever machinations the fanatical hatred of His enemies could devise. His body would bear the marks of their cruelties and His heart would sustain betrayal, calumny and insult, but nothing would or could prevent Him from carrying out His God-appointed mission.

Great efforts were made to obtain His release. His sister made personal intercessions with the Shah for her brother's life. Some of His highly-placed friends managed to have set up a number of tribunals, all of which established His innocence of the attempted assassination; His brothers and near kindred were unrelaxing in their efforts, and a certain Mullá, surnamed 'Azím, publicly confessed to his own complicity in the plot and completely exonerated Bahá'u'lláh. Several times His release was authorized, but the 'ulamá prevented it. Eventually it was the decisive intervention of the Russian Minister which accomplished it, a service which Bahá'u'lláh acknowledged later in His letter to the Czar (see Chapter 14).

The Grand Vizier obtained the monarch's reluctant consent to Bahá'u'lláh's release and dispatched his representatives to the Síyáh-Chál to fetch Him. Disdaining the clean garments which were offered Him, He appeared before the members of the imperial government in His prison garb. Appalled at the sight He thus presented, the Grand Vizier addressed Him: 'Had you chosen to take my advice, and had you dissociated yourself from the Faith of the Siyyid-i-Báb, you would never have suffered the pains and indignities that have been heaped upon you.'

Bahá'u'lláh replied, 'Had you, in your turn, followed My counsels, the affairs of the government would not have reached so critical a stage.'

'What is it that you advise me now to do?' the Prime Minister enquired.

'Command the governors of the realm to cease shedding the blood of the innocent, to cease plundering their property, to cease dishonouring their women, and injuring their children', was the instant reply.

The Grand Vizier acted at once on that advice, but his instructions proved to be only temporarily and to a negligible degree obeyed.[1]

What joy, relief and gratitude flooded the hearts of Navváb and her children when their beloved was restored to them! What grief as they saw the marks of the chains on His neck and the wounded feet still unhealed after the bastinado and the stocks. Their devoted attention to His recovery of health was given short shrift. Hardly had they been reunited when the Shah's decree of banishment was received. Bahá'u'lláh was given one month to leave Persian territory forever and was allowed to choose the land of His exile.

The Russian Minister immediately offered the protection of his government and every assistance for Bahá'u'lláh and His family to settle in Russia. Bahá'u'lláh graciously declined and chose to settle in Baghdad. Iraq at that time was under Turkish rule, the Sultan being also the all-powerful Caliph of Sunni Islam; Persia was and is overwhelmingly Shi'ah.*

The journey from Teheran to Baghdad, a distance of some four hundred miles, would take three months. It would be made in the depth of winter, over the snow-covered mountains of western Persia. Bahá'u'lláh, despoiled of all His vast wealth,

---

* Islam and western Christianity alike are split into two major divisions with hundreds of sub-divisions and minor sects in each religion.

not yet convalescent from the rigours of the Síyáh-Chál, was in no position to prepare properly for such a journey, and the government's provision was markedly inadequate. Several commentators have voiced the opinion that this was deliberate policy, pursued in the hope that the distinguished captive, enfeebled and destitute, would succumb to the hardships entailed.

On January 12th, 1853 the caravan set out from Teheran: Bahá'u'lláh; Navváb, riding in a sort of howdah borne on a mule; 'Abdu'l-Bahá, the eldest son, a boy of nine; Bahíyyih Khánum, the daughter, aged seven; and two of Bahá'u'lláh's brothers, Mírzá Músá and Mírzá Muhammad-Qulí, who remained loyal to Him to the end of their lives. The third child, Mírzá Mihdí, but two years old and delicate, was left in the care of his maternal great-grandmother until it became propitious for him to rejoin his parents. This little band of exiles was escorted from their native land by an officer of the Persian imperial bodyguard and an official representing the Russian Legation.

In spite of little food, no comforts, inadequate protection against the cold, any hopes His enemies may have entertained were doomed to disappointment. The exiles all survived the perils of that journey and arrived in Baghdad on April 8th, 1853. Among many incidents during its course – poignant, heartbreaking, uplifting – one is selected for the light it casts upon Bahá'u'lláh and the influence He exerted. The Governor of Karand, a town on Persian territory but close to the Iraqi border, extended a 'warm and enthusiastic reception' to the travellers. 'He was shown, in return, such kindness by Bahá'u'lláh that the people of the entire village were affected, and continued, long after, to extend such hospitality to His followers on their way to Baghdád that they gained the reputation of being known as Bábís.'[2]

In a meditation composed during the course of that terrible journey, Bahá'u'lláh revealed:

My God, My Master, My Desire! . . . Thou hast created this atom of dust through the consummate power of Thy might, and nurtured Him with Thine hands which none can chain up . . . Thou hast destined for Him trials and tribulations which no tongue can describe, nor any of Thy Tablets adequately recount. The throat Thou didst accustom to the touch of silk Thou hast, in the end, clasped with strong chains, and the body Thou didst ease with brocades and velvets Thou hast at last subjected to the abasement of a dungeon. Thy decree hath shackled Me with unnumbered fetters, and cast about My neck chains that none can sunder. A number of years have passed during which afflictions have, like showers of mercy, rained upon me . . . How many the nights during which the weight of chains and fetters allowed Me no rest, and how numerous the days during which peace and tranquillity were denied Me, by reason of that wherewith the hands and tongues of men have afflicted Me! Both bread and water which Thou hast through Thy all-embracing mercy, allowed unto the beasts of the field, they have, for a time, forbidden unto this servant, and the things they refused to inflict upon such as have seceded from Thy Cause, the same have they suffered to be inflicted upon Me, until, finally, Thy decree was irrevocably fixed, and Thy behest summoned this servant to depart out of Persia, accompanied by a number of frail-bodied men and children of tender age, at this time when the cold is so intense that one cannot even speak, and ice and snow so abundant that it is impossible to move.[3]

This cruel episode ended on a happier note. The first encampment, after the border with Iraq had been crossed, was in a flower-strewn orchard of orange trees and date palms. Its streams reflected the sunlight and birds were singing. As they came to this blessed resting place Bahá'u'lláh told His companions that all His enemies' hopes and plans had come to naught.

But this was no portent of better days.

When Bahá'u'lláh came out of the prison He was, for all that the world knew, still a Bábí. Not even to His closest kin did He confide the secret that burned within Him, and He would not make a public declaration of His mission until ten years had elapsed.

Many years later Bahíyyih Khánum related that there was an inner radiance about Him and Shoghi Effendi states in *God Passes By* that a 'few of His fellow-disciples, distinguished by their sagacity, and their personal attachment and devotion to Him, perceived the radiance of the as yet unrevealed glory that had flooded His soul, and would have, but for His restraining influence, divulged His secret and proclaimed it far and wide'.[4]

The Báb had designated Bahá'u'lláh's half-brother Mírzá Yaḥyá as the nominal head of the Bábí community, a move that was seen by the more perceptive as providing some slight protection to Bahá'u'lláh, whom the Báb knew to be 'He whom God shall make manifest' and to whom He sent, just before His martyrdom, His pens, seals and papers.

Despite the advantages of his background, Yaḥyá was weak, cowardly, inordinately ambitious and entirely bereft of any qualities of leadership. After the martyrdom of the Báb, and even during His imprisonment before that heroic event, Yaḥyá had gone into hiding in fear of his life in various disguises, forbidding the Bábís to recognize him, speak to him in public or disclose his whereabouts. It was to Bahá'u'lláh that they turned for guidance, support and encouragement. When He was arrested and imprisoned, the one remaining figure among the followers of the Báb with sufficient authority and character to provide the leadership so desperately needed, was effectively removed. Shepherdless, proscribed, exhausted, their plight was indeed piteous.

Their one hope was the advent of 'He whom God shall make manifest', for whom the Báb and thousands of their fellow-believers had sacrificed their lives. The Báb had clearly indicated that His appearance was imminent – many were told that they would see Him; all should prepare for His coming. This expectancy now became the focus of their thoughts, their prayers, their prospect of life. So imperative was their need and their longing that a few even made the stupendous claim to be that One. The tragic fantasy of such claims was a measure of their desperation and of the spiritual decline which was afflicting them.

One of these claimants was Siyyid Muḥammad-i-Iṣfáhání, later to emerge as the antichrist of the Bahá'í Revelation. Motivated by inordinate ambition, he saw himself as the head of the Bábí community – the 'King of the Bayán'* as he is reported to have styled himself. He recognized in the nomination of Yaḥyá the opportunity to achieve his ambition. By flattery and by fostering Yaḥyá's unfounded claim to be the Báb's successor, he easily dominated the vain and credulous Yaḥyá and beguiled him into plots and intrigues and criminal acts, not stopping at murder.

Bahá'u'lláh, arrived in Baghdad, took up the task He had vowed, while in the darkness of the Síyáh-Chál, to undertake. He would arise for the regeneration of the hapless Bábí community, bludgeoned, homeless, leaderless, with no recourse to justice or human rights. A number of these pitiful victims had fled to Baghdad and its environs, seeking safety. They were indeed in need of rehabilitation: disillusioned, sunk in distress of mind and spirit with no guide of sufficient authority to cheer their hearts, resolve their doubts or reunite them and restore their self-respect. Bahá'u'lláh now faced this herculean labour, only to find Himself confronted by the intrigues of Mírzá Yaḥyá, egged on and manipulated by Siyyid Muḥammad.

Bahá'u'lláh respected the Báb's nomination and responded to all Yaḥyá's animosity with forbearance and patience. In earlier days He had, at the written request of the Báb, provided for Yaḥyá's education and upbringing, and on the notorious occasion in Ámul when He and His companions were arrested and condemned to the bastinado, Bahá'u'lláh intervened on Yaḥyá's behalf pleading that he was but one of His attendants. He offered Himself as a scapegoat for the whole party and suffered the torture until his feet bled.[5]

He now complied with Yaḥyá's request for a sum of money

---

* The Báb's book is called the *Bayán*.

which enabled him to maintain his cowardly incognito and to set up in Baghdad as a salesman of shrouds.

Bahá'u'lláh's ascendancy was such that large numbers of Bábís and others began to flock to His presence. His moral grandeur and exaltation of spirit drew people to Him from all strata of society, eager to sun themselves in the radiance which emanated from Him and to enjoy the upliftment which all experienced in His presence. Signs of the unity and former fervour of the Bábís began to reappear, and as the news of Bahá'u'lláh's growing influence began to percolate back to Persia, more and more of the persecuted Bábís came to Baghdad to seek His shelter.

All this was fuel to the unbridled hatred and jealousy of Siyyid Muḥammad, who set out to destroy Bahá'u'lláh. He recruited a band of ruffians to attack people in the streets, to break into the holy shrines and steal the ornaments, to create disturbances in the bazaar and to lay all these outrages to the charge of the Bábís. Yaḥyá engaged in a campaign of secret vilifications, intrigues and machinations against the exiles and those gathering around them. His insinuations, spread by letters and gossip-mongers, attempted to portray Bahá'u'lláh as a usurper.

This campaign, aimed at nullifying Bahá'u'lláh's benign intent, increasing the doubts and confusion which had so ravaged the beaten community, and bringing it into disrepute with the authorities, began to endanger the Faith of the Báb. Every exhortation and advice which flowed from Bahá'u'lláh's pen was misinterpreted, challenged and criticized, and an abortive attempt was made to injure Him physically. All His efforts to remedy a desperate situation were being frustrated and made the cause of greater disunity. There was but one solution, and Bahá'u'lláh took it.

On the morning of April 10th, 1854 His family arose to find Him gone.

Chapter 9

DARVÍSH
MUḤAMMAD-I-ÍRÁNÍ

B AHÁ'U'LLÁH'S retirement to the remote uplands of
Kurdistán recalls similar occasions in the lives of the
Manifestations of God. The stay of Moses in the desert
of Paran, the years of meditation of Gautama Buddha, the
forty days and nights of Jesus in the wilderness, the retreats of
Muhammad to the caves of Mount Hira are all regarded as
periods of preparation for their world-shaking tasks. In view of
the distressing circumstances prevailing in Baghdad and the
reluctance of Bahá'u'lláh to declare as yet His mission, we are
not surprised to read from His pen,

The one object of Our retirement was to avoid becoming a subject
of discord among the faithful, a source of disturbance unto our
companions, the means of injury to any soul, or the cause of sorrow
to any heart. [1]

Disguised as a dervish, roughly clad, on foot and with but
one attendant, Bahá'u'lláh under the assumed name of Darvísh
Muhammad-i-Íráni set out upon the two-hundred-mile journey
to the north-eastern part of Iraq on the frontier with Persia, a
wild and mountainous region 'whose sturdy and warlike
people were known for their age-long hostility to the Persians,
whom they regarded as seceders from the Faith of Islám, and
from whom they differed in their outlook, race and language'. [2]

We sought shelter upon the summit of a remote mountain which lay at some three days' distance from the nearest human habitation. The comforts of life were completely lacking. We remained entirely isolated from Our fellow men . . .[3]

The birds of the air were My companions and the beasts of the field My associates . . .[4]

Many a night We had no food for sustenance, and many a day Our body found no rest.[5]

His companion, Áqá Abu'l-Qásim, returning from a trading visit to Persia, was set upon by bandits and killed, and Bahá'u'lláh was entirely alone.

The mountain which gave Him shelter was Sar-Galú, on whose summit, as well as in one of its caves, He spent much of the two years of His retirement. From 'a rude structure, made of stone',[6] used by peasants of the region during their visits in spring and autumn, He roamed the wilderness alone and unaided in His struggle to accommodate to the awesome station and mission to which He was summoned. He testified in later years

From Our eyes there rained tears of anguish, and in Our bleeding heart surged an ocean of agonizing pain.[7]

And yet

By Him Who hath My being between His hands! notwithstanding these showers of afflictions and unceasing calamities, Our soul was wrapt in blissful joy, and Our whole being evinced an ineffable gladness. For in Our solitude We were unaware of the harm or benefit, the health or ailment, of any soul. Alone, We communed with Our spirit, oblivious of the world and all that is therein.[8]

Shoghi Effendi, writing of those days, referred to 'the odes He revealed, whilst wrapped in His devotions during those days of utter seclusion . . . the prayers and soliloquies which, in verse and prose, both in Arabic and Persian, poured from His sorrow-laden soul, many of which He was wont to chant aloud to Himself, at dawn and during the watches of the night . . .'[9]

He described them as 'the forerunners of those immortal works — the *Kitáb-i-Íqán*, the *Hidden Words* and the *Seven Valleys* — which in the years preceding His Declaration in Baghdád, were to enrich so vastly the steadily swelling volume of His writings, and which paved the way for a further flowering of His prophetic genius in His epoch-making Proclamation to the world, couched in the form of mighty Epistles to the kings and rulers of mankind, and finally for the last fruition of His Mission in the Laws and Ordinances of His Dispensation formulated during His confinement in the Most Great Prison of 'Akká'.[10]

The chain of events which led to the termination of Bahá'u'lláh's isolation is strongly reminiscent of those interventions of divine Providence, which, in the very earliest days of the Báb's ministry, had guided some of the Letters of the Living to His presence and on certain occasions had preserved the infant Faith from irretrievable disaster.

One night in a dream the Prophet Muhammad appeared to a certain Shaykh of Sulaymáníyyih and directed him to seek out Darvísh Muhammad-i-Íraní. The Shaykh followed his visionary instructions and thus was made the first breach in Bahá'u'lláh's utter isolation and the first intimation that the itinerant dervish from Persia was possibly more than He appeared. At about the same time the following incident occurred, described by Lady Blomfield in her book *The Chosen Highway*. She had received the story from Bahá'u'lláh's daughter Bahíyyih Khánum, during her visits to the ladies of 'Abdu'l-Bahá's household in Haifa in 1921 and 1929.

A young boy, making his way to school in Sulaymáníyyih, in great trouble with tears streaming down his face, suddenly saw before him a dignified man who enquired, 'Why do you cry little boy?'

The boy explained, 'My teacher set our class some copy and I have lost mine. My teacher will be angry.'

'Dry your tears little boy,' said Bahá'u'lláh, for He it was, 'and I will set a copy for you.'

Bahá'u'lláh wrote a few lines and gave them to the boy, who ran off happy and grateful.

He showed the lines to his teacher who immediately asked, 'Where did you get this script? It is of royal penmanship.'

The little boy told his story and the piece of writing was shown with wonder to the students and instructors of the seminary. It came to the attention of Shaykh Ismá'íl, the leader of the Order which owned the seminary.

It was the perfection of the calligraphy in this small sample of Bahá'u'lláh's penmanship which aroused the curiosity of the learned. So excited was Shaykh Ismá'íl by this indication of unsuspected capacities and qualities in a lowly dervish that he himself, the leader of one of the most revered Orders in Sulaymáníyyih, set out at the head of a delegation consisting of that Order's 'most eminent doctors and distinguished students' to call on Darvísh Muhammad and probe the mystery surrounding him.[11]

As on every similar occasion in the life of Bahá'u'lláh, His genuine friendliness, allied to the unassuming majesty which surrounded Him, won the hearts of His visitors. His willingness to answer all their questions, in the course of which they glimpsed a depth of perception and wisdom beyond anything they had ever imagined, aroused their instant admiration, an attitude which only increased with their continuing visits. So attached did Shaykh Ismá'íl become to Him that he persisted in asking Him to reside in Sulaymáníyyih. After repeated requests Bahá'u'lláh consented and Darvísh Muhammad left his wild retreat and moved to a room in the seminary of the Order headed by Shaykh Ismá'íl.

His mounting ascendancy and fame attracted 'an increasing number of the 'ulamás, the scholars, the shaykhs, the doctors, the holy men and princes who had congregated in the seminaries of Sulaymáníyyih and Karkúk', who waited on Him daily, listening with delight to His discourses and resolutions of abstruse matters in their philosophy. The wide vistas which He opened to their minds released their imagination and evoked expressions of wonder and awe. 'Such was the esteem and respect entertained for Him that some held Him as One of the "men of the Unseen", others accounted Him an adept in alchemy and the science of divination, still others designated Him "a pivot of the universe", whilst a not inconsiderable number among His admirers went so far as to believe that His station was no less than that of a prophet. Kurds, Arabs, and Persians, learned and illiterate, both high and low, young and old, who had come to know Him, regarded Him with equal reverence, and not a few among them with genuine and profound affection, and this despite certain assertions and allusions to His station He had made in public, which, had they fallen from the lips of any other member of His race, would have provoked such fury as to endanger His life.'[12]

'Abdu'l-Bahá related of this episode: 'In a short time Kurdistán was magnetized with His love. During this period Bahá'u'lláh lived in poverty. His garments were those of the poor and needy. His food was that of the indigent and lowly. An atmosphere of majesty haloed Him as the sun at midday. Everywhere He was greatly revered and loved.'[13]

The fame of Bahá'u'lláh inevitably spread beyond the confines of Sulaymáníyyih and quickly reached Baghdad. The coincidence of Abu'l-Qásim being missed at the same time as Bahá'u'lláh had been noted, and since he was able, as he lay dying, to breathe his name and say that all his money and effects belonged to Darvísh Muhammad-i-Írání, the strong suspicion that the exalted personage reported in Sulaymáníyyih could be none other than Bahá'u'lláh was amply confirmed.

'Abdu'l-Bahá, but twelve years old, and Mírzá Músá, Bahá'u'lláh's brother, immediately dispatched Shaykh Sultán, Mírzá Músá's father-in-law and a devoted, staunch Bábí, attended by one faithful believer, to Sulaymáníyyih to find Bahá'u'lláh and beg Him to return. They did find Him and He did return.

Thus did the divine will operate through the influence of a dream and the apparently fortuitous discovery of a piece of calligraphy; the Cause of God was rescued from an ignominious dissolution and its chief protagonist set out on His world-encompassing mission.

Shaykh Sultán related to Nabíl, the famed historian of the Báb's Dispensation, that when he arrived in Sulaymáníyyih and discovered Bahá'u'lláh in the seminary, 'I found all those who lived with Him in that place, from the Master down to the humblest neophytes, so enamoured of and carried away by their love for Bahá'u'lláh, and so unprepared to contemplate the possibility of His departure that I felt certain that were I to inform them of the purpose of my visit, they would not have hesitated to put an end to my life.'[14]

In that passage of the *Kitáb-i-Íqán*, already quoted, in which Bahá'u'lláh stated the reason for His retirement to the wilderness, He also stated that He contemplated no return. Later in that same passage He explained that when summoned to return, he surrendered His own will to God.

Chapter 10
RETURN TO BAGHDAD

RETURNING to Baghdad astride the 'River of Tribulation', Baghdad which had been the centre of the civilized world when Europe was emerging from its Dark Ages but was now the decayed capital of a province in the empire of the Ottoman Turks, Bahá'u'lláh confided to His travelling companion, Shaykh Sultán, that the days of that journey were the last of 'peace and tranquillity' He would ever experience.[1]

While He was away the fortunes of the Bábí community had sunk to their lowest ebb, and the Faith of the Báb was approaching the verge of extinction. The criminal pursuits of Yahyá and Siyyid Muhammad had resulted in the Bábís being regarded with such opprobrium and contempt that individuals were vilified and assaulted in the bazaar, while the Cause with which they were identified was openly reviled. The situation had come to such a pass that even Yahyá, realizing that there was no future for himself under such conditions, had added his entreaties to those of the few steadfast members of the community begging Bahá'u'lláh to return.

So great was the sadness which engulfed Bahá'u'lláh as He realized the position, that He remained in His home for several days. Then He arose for the regeneration of the Bábí community, and once again the same process of mounting ascendancy and influence which had unfolded in Iran and Sulaymáníyyih rapidly evolved in Baghdad, but this time on a larger scale and with far greater results.

Bahá'u'lláh's presence in Baghdad at once provided the

demoralized community with the firm centre of authority it
so badly needed. Although He had not yet revealed Himself
as 'Him Who God shall make manifest' and would not do so
for another seven years, the Bábís recognized in Him their true
Counsellor, capable of restoring the prestige and ensuring the
stability of the Faith. They turned to Him with gratitude and
renewed hope. Many even of the twenty-five who had advanced
claims during His absence went to Him in repentance and
were forgiven. Devoted believers, seeking refuge from the
bitter persecutions in Iran only to meet disillusionment and
despair under Yaḥyá's disastrous influence, prepared to return.
Hearing now that Bahá'u'lláh was in Baghdad they flocked to
Him, bringing their loyalty, gratitude and joy to the rehabili-
tated community. Their numbers were greatly increased by
streams of other Persian Bábís who journeyed to Baghdad for
the sole purpose of attaining the presence of Bahá'u'lláh,
whence they returned to their country to spread the news of
His growing eminence and to carry to their fellow believers
the regenerating power of His spirit and wise counsels. Nor
was the curiosity of the leaders of Baghdad society in the least
diminished by the appearance of large numbers of his bereft
admirers from Sulaymáníyyih flocking to their city 'with the
name of "Darvísh Muḥammad" on their lips and the "house
of Mírzá Músá the Bábí" as their goal'. The leaders of the city,
including the Muftí, began to call on Him and were quickly
enrolled in the growing band of His admirers. 'The house . . .
to which Bahá'u'lláh's family had moved prior to His return
from Kurdistán, had now become the focal centre of a great
number of seekers, visitors and pilgrims, including Kurds,
Persians, Arabs and Turks, and derived from the Muslim, the
Jewish and Christian Faiths. It had, moreover, become a
veritable sanctuary to which the victims of the injustice of the
official representative of the Persian government were wont to
flee, in the hope of securing redress for the wrongs they had
suffered . . . fugitives, driven by the ever-present fear of
persecution, sought, with their wives and children, the relative

security afforded them by close proximity to One who had already become the rallying point for the members of a sorely-vexed community. Persians of high eminence, living in exile, rejecting, in the face of the mounting prestige of Bahá'u'lláh, the dictates of moderation and prudence, sat, forgetful of their pride, at His feet, and imbibed, each according to his capacity, a measure of His spirit and wisdom . . . Nor was the then representative of the British government, Colonel Sir Arnold Burrows Kemball, Consul-General in Baghdád, insensible of the position which Bahá'u'lláh now occupied. Entering into friendly correspondence with Him, he, as testified by Bahá'u'lláh Himself, offered Him the protection of British citizenship, called on Him in person, and undertook to transmit to Queen Victoria any communication He might wish to forward to her. He even expressed his readiness to arrange for the transfer of His residence to India, or to any place agreeable to Him. This suggestion Bahá'u'lláh declined, choosing to abide in the dominions of the Sultán of Turkey.'[2] There has been speculation as to the reasons for this choice by Bahá'u'lláh. Some have suggested that the fulfilment of the prophecies about the Promised One may have been a factor. It is certainly difficult to imagine how He would have come to the Holy Land had He been resident in a British territory and accepted its citizenship. However there is no authentication for such a view, rational as it may seem.

The moral transformation which Bahá'u'lláh had effected in the character and behaviour of the Bábí community both in Baghdad and throughout Persia, as well as His own mounting prestige and spiritual eminence, inevitably kindled anew the glowing hatred of His implacable and inveterate enemies, the Muslim religious leaders, both Sunni and Shi'ah. Opposed to any ideas of reform or the slightest diminution of their personal power, which extended to life and death, they were the embodiment of that fanaticism, clothed in religious garb, which had always attempted to obliterate the new message from God, brought by the Founders of the world's religions.

Their constant efforts were directed towards persuading the Turkish authorities to hand over Bahá'u'lláh and His companions to Persian authority or to extradite them to Persia where they could be dealt with once and for all. Bahá'u'lláh frustrated this scheme by obtaining for Himself and His exiled companions Turkish citizenship. This was obtained with the delighted support of Námiq Páshá, the Governor of the province, who had become so enamoured of Bahá'u'lláh and held Him in such high esteem that he called upon Him personally to express his veneration.

Many and varied are the stories of remarkable incidents which occurred during the seven years intervening between Bahá'u'lláh's return from Kurdistán and the declaration of His mission on the eve of His second exile. They all testify to the grandeur, the exaltation, the radiance of His being, the compassion and love which flowed from Him to His fellow men, His ability to reconcile enemies, to comfort the poor, uphold the downtrodden, and inspire the powerful with intent of justice and benevolence. At all times He was superior to the machinations of His enemies, disregarding their futile plots and criminal attempts to destroy Him.

On one occasion a known criminal, Ridá by name, was commissioned to assassinate Him while He paced the bank of the Tigris. As Bahá'u'lláh approached him this man became so agitated that he dropped his pistol and remained confused and helpless. Bahá'u'lláh requested Mírzá Músá, who accompanied Him, to pick up the gun, return it to the would-be assassin and point out the way to his home. 'He seems to have lost his way,' He said. This same Ridá, on a previous occasion, had entered the public bath with a pistol hidden in his clothing, intending to kill Bahá'u'lláh, but upon confronting Him his courage deserted him and he fled.

The Bábís were well aware of such dangers from their malevolent enemies. They maintained an all-night guard round Bahá'u'lláh's house and kept what observation they could on Him. He would have no bodyguard and once frustrated a plot whereby some of the lower elements of the population were to affront Him and provoke an incident, by approaching them, letting them know He was aware of their intention, joking with them and leaving them in confusion.

The conversation of some of the princes who visited Him, reclining on the crude furniture of the humble room in which visitors were received, is very instructive. They were all puzzled that such a poorly-furnished and simple room could be a place of such wonderful happiness which everyone who entered it experienced. One of the Persian Princes said he would build a duplicate of it in his own home. When Bahá'u'lláh heard this He smiled and said that the Prince could no doubt make an exact copy of that low-roofed, modest room, but what of his ability to open onto it the spiritual doors leading to the hidden worlds of God?[3]

Another Prince said, 'I know not how to explain it; were all the sorrows of the world to be crowded into my heart they would, I feel, all vanish, when in the presence of Bahá'u'lláh. It is as if I had entered Paradise itself.'[4]

Bahá'u'lláh shared the state of poverty which circumstances had forced upon the exiles. Whatever sums of money came to Him were largely distributed to the poor and used in making small gifts of tea or such to neighbours and friends. Describing His life at that time He recalled that He had no change of linen and that His one shirt would be washed and dried and worn again. Far from lowering Him in the estimation of the people, such austerity only added to the grandeur and majesty of His Person.

One particularly moving incident reveals the genuine love and friendliness which flowed from His heart, particularly to the helpless and downtrodden. An old woman, eighty years of age, living in a ruined house, waited for Him every day as He made His way to a coffee-house. Bahá'u'lláh would greet her, ask after her health and give her some money. She would kiss His hands and wanted to kiss His face but was too short to reach Him. He bent down to allow her to do so. His later comment, 'She knows that I like her, that is why she likes Me', reveals the genuineness of His bounty and compassion. Before leaving Baghdad He arranged a daily allowance for her to the end of her days.*

Bahá'u'lláh walked the streets and quarters of Baghdad, regardless of the plots against His safety and very life. 'Many and moving are the testimonies of bystanders who were privileged to gaze on His countenance, observe His gait, or overhear His remarks, as He moved through the lanes and streets of the city, or paced the banks of the river; of the worshippers who watched Him pray in their mosques; of the mendicant, the sick, the aged, and the unfortunate whom He succored, healed, supported and comforted; of the visitors, from the haughtiest prince to the meanest beggar, who crossed His threshold and sat at His feet; of the merchant, the artisan, and the shopkeeper who waited upon Him and supplied His daily needs; of His devotees who had perceived the signs of His hidden glory; of His adversaries who were confounded or disarmed by the power of His utterance and the warmth of His love; of the priests and laymen, the noble and learned, who besought Him with the intention of either challenging His authority, or testing His knowledge, or investigating His claims, or confessing their shortcomings, or declaring their conversion to the Cause He had espoused.'[5]

It is difficult for western people to realize the extent of the tremendous powers wielded even today by the religious leaders of Islam. The days in Europe when the Pope could excommunicate and depose the kings of Christendom and the Inquisition could order the torture and execution of heretics are long gone and forgotten. Not so in Islam. In many Muslim countries the religious leaders still wield extraordinary power. Even those of less than the highest rank may decree death and imprisonment and launch jihad or holy war against whomsoever

* This incident is given by H. M. Balyuzi in his *Bahá'u'lláh, The King of Glory.* Oxford: George Ronald, 1980.

they consider to be infidels. Only yesterday the Ayatollahs of Iran deposed the Shah and even now are barely restrained from exterminating the Bahá'ís of that country, from whom they still withhold normal human rights. In Bahá'u'lláh's days these powers were virtually unlimited,* and were vested in a horde of ignorant, prejudiced 'ulamá who preyed upon the remnants of the once-glorious civilization of Islam. Any threat to their entrenched privileges and powers would be met with instant, violent suppression, as had already been seen in their inhuman treatment of the illustrious Báb and thousands of His dedicated followers.

Baghdad, Karbila, Najaf and Kazimayn formed together a veritable stronghold of Shi'ah Islam, the site of many of its holy places, religious schools and endowments, and the residences of some of its most powerful and renowned leaders. Shoghi Effendi has described the critical situation which arose from the 'range and magnificence of Bahá'u'lláh's rising power' as 'a trial of strength between the growing brilliance of His glory and the dark and embattled forces of religious fanaticism'.[6]

The prime source of the jealousies and hatreds which were revivified by the growing strength of the reborn Bábí community was a certain Shaykh 'Abdu'l-Husayn who had been sent by the Shah to repair the holy sites in Karbila. Consumed by hatred of Bahá'u'lláh, he set out to destroy Him. He co-opted to his service the newly-arrived Persian consul-general, of lesser capacity than himself and a confirmed drunkard, who soon became his willing tool.

Their first foray against Bahá'u'lláh was aimed at having Him and His companions extradited to Persia, an endeavour which was defeated, as we have seen, by Bahá'u'lláh's vigorous action and the loving admiration conceived for Him by the new governor, Námiq Páshá. The Shaykh's next attempt was to spread abroad the tale of a number of dreams which he

---

* For a detailed account of the venality, corruption, degradation and decay which resulted from such a condition see Lord Curzon's *Persia and the Persian Question*.

claimed to have had and which he interpreted to his own aggrandizement and the denigration of Bahá'u'lláh. Bahá'u'lláh reinterpreted these dreams to the great disadvantage of the Shaykh who was advised to seek an interview with Bahá'u'lláh so that he could see for himself the stature of the person he sought to destroy. To this he agreed but when Bahá'u'lláh consented to receive him, his courage failed and he did not keep the appointment. This ignominious outcome only served to increase his resentment and hatred.

Next he planned through his minion, the consul-general, the public assault upon Bahá'u'lláh already described. This too failed when Bahá'u'lláh confronted the would-be assailants. It was this consul who commissioned the assassin Ridá and provided him with the pistol which he so affrightedly dropped.

'Abdu'l-Ḥusayn now conceived a new plan for the extradition of Bahá'u'lláh. He composed, and sent in swift succession to members of the Shah's court, lengthy and utterly false reports of Bahá'u'lláh's intention to overthrow the monarchy. He presented, in greatly exaggerated terms, a non-existent political purpose to His ascendancy, saying that He had won the allegiance of the Iraqi tribesmen and could mobilize immediately an army of a hundred thousand well-armed troops with which he intended to launch, in conjunction with several leaders inside Persia, an insurrection against the Shah. The viziers, courtiers and sycophants surrounding the Shah were not greatly disposed to discredit or rebut such unfounded accusations, and that monarch was persuaded to give a mandate to Shaykh 'Abdu'l-Ḥusayn conferring on him full powers and requiring the Persian 'ulamá and officials in Iraq to render him every assistance.

The Shaykh at once sent copies of this mandate to the religious leaders in Najaf and Karbila, and summoned them to a conference at his residence in Kazimayn. 'A concourse of shaykhs, mullás and mujtahids, eager to curry favour with the sovereign, promptly responded.'[7] They resolved to launch a jihad (holy war) against the Bábís and by a sudden assault

exterminate the community in Baghdad and thus destroy the
Faith of the Báb at its heart. Shaykh 'Abdu'l-Husayn must
have rejoiced, assured that his hopes were at last to be realized.
But he was doomed once again to failure.

Their infamous plan foundered on the rock of the noble
character of Shaykh Murtidáy-i-Ansárí, the leading mujtahid
of the Shi'ah world. Renowned for his undeviating sense of
justice, he refused to pronounce sentence against the Bábís.
He left the gathering, sent a message to Bahá'u'lláh expressing
regret for what had happened, and returned to his home.

The frustrated 'ulamá, far from mending their ways, now
conceived yet another plan which, once more, would bring
them only scorn and contempt and increase still further
Bahá'u'lláh's ascendancy.

Frequently Bahá'u'lláh entertained at His house mixed
groups of Muslim divines, Jewish rabbis, Christians and a few
European scholars. At these meetings each person was encour-
aged to put questions to Bahá'u'lláh or to ask for comment on
abstruse matters, and although from such varied backgrounds,
they invariably received satisfying answers. One of these
meetings took place at the time of Shaykh 'Abdu'l-Husayn's
conference. Unchastened and unabashed, they deputized 'the
learned and devout Hájí Mullá Hasan-i-'Ammú'[8] to attend
Bahá'u'lláh's meeting, put certain questions to Him and
when, as was expected, completely satisfactory answers were
given, he was to issue what they considered an unanswerable
challenge. All went as foreseen. Mullá Hasan stated that the
'ulamá recognized the vastness of Bahá'u'lláh's knowledge and
virtue, in which He had no peer, that He had never acquired this
knowledge through study, but that His wisdom and righteousness were not sufficient proof of the truth of His mission. They
therefore asked Him to perform a miracle which would
completely satisfy and tranquillize their hearts. Bahá'u'lláh's
reply was:

Although you have no right to ask this, for God should test His creatures, and they should not test God, still I allow and accept this request. But the Cause of God is not a theatrical display that is presented every hour, of which some new diversion may be asked for every day. If it were thus, the Cause of God would become mere child's play.

The 'ulamá must therefore assemble and with one accord choose one miracle, and write that after the performance of this miracle they will no longer entertain doubts about Me, and that all will acknowledge and confess the truth of my Cause. Let them seal this paper and bring it to Me. This must be the accepted criterion: If the miracle is performed, no doubt will remain for them; and if not, we shall be convicted of imposture.[9]

Mullá Ḥasan arose instantly, kissed the knee of Bahá'u'lláh and left to deliver his message. The 'ulamá, disconcerted, spent three days discussing what to do and then decided to let the matter drop. They argued that Bahá'u'lláh was a sorceror and might well perform some enchantment, which would leave them helpless. Mullá Ḥasan felt so embarrassed that he could not go to Bahá'u'lláh again; he sent the reply by messenger and added, 'I am ashamed of the behaviour of my colleagues.'[10]

'Abdu'l-Bahá, commenting on this episode, declared it to be unique in the religious history of mankind and called attention to a similar challenge made by Bahá'u'lláh to the Shah in His Lawḥ-i-Sulṭán (Letter to the Shah): 'Gather the 'ulamá and summon Me, that the evidences and proofs may be established.'[11]

Mullá Ḥasan gave wide publicity to this incident, speaking about it in the holy cities of Iráq and throughout Persia, always stressing the fear of the 'ulamá and their refusal to take up the challenge.

Ever since Bahá'u'lláh and His companions had obtained Turkish citizenship, which gave them some protection from the Persian fanatics, the government in Teheran had initiated a vigorous campaign at the Sublime Porte to induce the Sultan to issue a decree of extradition to Persia or to remove the exiles further from the Persian border. Through their ambassador in Istanbul they represented Bahá'u'lláh as the leader of a 'misguided and detestable sect', secretly corrupting and misleading foolish persons and ignorant weaklings,* a source of mischief among the streams of pilgrims who flocked to the holy places of Shi'ah Islam in the neighbourhood of Baghdad. While Sultán 'Abdu'l-Majíd occupied the throne their hopes were constantly dashed, since that monarch preferred to rely on the favourable reports which he received from his governors in Baghdad, rather than on those of the Persian ambassador. He died in 1861 and 'Abdu'l-'Azíz acceded to the throne. The Persians immediately redoubled their pressure on the new Sultan, salting their request with reference to a 'friendly power' and eventually 'Abdu'l-'Azíz was induced to issue a decree inviting Bahá'u'lláh, His family and some of His followers to Constantinople.

Námiq Páshá, the Governor of Baghdad, among the most fervent of Bahá'u'lláh's admirers and the one who had secured Turkish citizenship and issued passports to the exiles, was so distressed by the order for Bahá'u'lláh's removal that he delayed three months, during which time he received five successive instructions from 'Alí Páshá, the Grand Vizier, to implement it. Finally in March 1863, unable to resist the duties of his office any longer, or to bring himself to deliver such a message in person, he arranged for his deputy to meet Bahá'u'lláh and show Him the original missive from 'Alí Páshá. H. M. Balyuzi states, 'it was an invitation to come to Istanbul that was presented to Bahá'u'lláh, definitely not a command, and He accepted in the spirit and the way it was offered'.[12] Shoghi Effendi confirms this in *God Passes By*, disclosing that it was 'couched in courteous language, inviting Bahá'u'lláh to proceed, as a guest of the Ottoman government, to Constantinople, placing a sum of money at His disposal,

---

* Can we not hear echoes of the first mention of the contemptible sect of the Nazarene?

and ordering a mounted escort to accompany Him for His protection'.[13]

Bahá'u'lláh assented to the removal but declined the sum of money. On being advised that such a refusal would offend the authorities He accepted it and immediately distributed it to the poor.

Towards the end of His stay in Baghdad He began to make reference to trials ahead. During the Naw-Rúz* celebrations in 1863 He revealed the *Tablet of the Holy Mariner* which foretold great tribulation and suffering for the Mariner Himself and the inhabitants of His ark. The day following the reading of this Tablet to the assembled believers, the Deputy-Governor delivered 'Alí Páshá's letter to Him.

The news of Bahá'u'lláh's further exile plunged the Bábí community of Baghdad into profound despair. They were overwhelmed by shock and a sense of tragedy. How could they forget their recent past when, bereft of the guidance of Bahá'u'lláh, they had plunged to the lowest depths of desperation and ignominy? They recognized whose guiding hand had renewed their spiritual health, restored their self-respect and raised them to honour among the citizens of an alien capital city. What would be their future without Him? Who would defend them against the assaults of a ruthless enemy? To whom could they direct the feelings of love and respect, awe and adoration which flooded their souls in His presence? The sense of the approaching separation from Him so appalled them that many resolved to take their own lives unless they were permitted to accompany Him, no matter to what further hardship and deprivation. As He once had regenerated their spiritual force, He now comforted their agitated hearts, calmed their fears and restored them to resignation with the will of God. To each one of them, 'Arab or Persian, man or woman, child or adult', living in Baghdad He gave a separate

---

* Naw-Rúz, the ancient new year's day of Zoroastrianism, is also the first day of the year in the calendar established by the Báb, March 21st the spring equinox.

Tablet in His own hand, in which He prepared them to remain steadfast in difficult troubles and crises ahead.

The preparations for Bahá'u'lláh's departure involved a mobilization of all the impedimenta of a major caravan — howdahs for the ladies and children and those unable to walk, all the equipment of daily living for about forty people over a period of four months. The site chosen for the point of departure was a garden belonging to Najíb Páshá, on the north bank of the Tigris on the outskirts of Baghdad. On the afternoon of April 22nd, 1863, Bahá'u'lláh entered the Najíbíyyih garden and remained there for twelve days. On the twelfth day the caravan comprising Bahá'u'lláh, His family, twenty-six of His disciples and the military escort set out on its historic journey across the uplands of Anatolia to the port of Samsun on the Black Sea, whence they were conveyed by steamer to the capital of the Turkish empire.

No greater testimony to Bahá'u'lláh's grandeur and majesty could be provided than the tumultuous scenes witnessed in Baghdad during the last days of His residence in that city. Over and beyond this, those twelve days, by reason of the stupendous events which transpired in that garden, came to be celebrated as the holiest and most significant of all Bahá'í festivals. It is forever known as the Festival of Riḍván and that garden as the Garden of Riḍván (Paradise). For it was there that Bahá'u'lláh at last declared to His companions the reality of His miṣsion, the news for which they had so long yearned, so eagerly expected. The heroic and soul-shattering ministry of the Báb had at last borne its destined fruit and 'He Whom God shall make manifest' stood before them, recognized, acclaimed and worshipped.

Before attempting to describe that world-shaking event, let us contemplate for a moment the signs and wonders of His ascendancy and the prophetic circumstances under which His declaration was made.

From the moment the news of the Sultan's decree was conveyed to Bahá'u'lláh it spread rapidly throughout the city, arousing a furore of activity amongst all ranks of its inhabitants such as Baghdad had rarely seen. Shoghi Effendi describes it in *God Passes By*: 'A concourse of people of both sexes and of every age, comprising friends and strangers, Arabs, Kurds and Persians, notables and clerics, officials and merchants, as well as many of the lower classes, the poor, the orphaned, the outcast, some surprised, others heartbroken, many tearful and apprehensive, a few impelled by curiosity or secret satisfaction, thronged the approaches of His house, eager to catch a final glimpse of One Who, for a decade, had, through precept and example, exercised so potent an influence on so large a number of the heterogeneous inhabitants of their city.

'Leaving for the last time, amidst weeping and lamentation . . . and dispensing on His way with a lavish hand a last alms to the poor He had so faithfully befriended, and uttering words of comfort to the disconsolate who besought Him on every side, He, at length, reached the banks of the river, and was ferried across, accompanied by His sons and amanuensis, to the Najíbíyyih Garden, situated on the opposite shore.'[14]

Before embarking He addressed the faithful friends surrounding Him:

O My companions, I entrust to your keeping this city of Baghdád, in the state ye now behold it, when from the eyes of friends and strangers alike, crowding its housetops, its streets and markets, tears like the rain of spring are flowing down, and I depart. With you it now rests to watch lest your deeds and conduct dim the flame of love that gloweth within the breasts of its inhabitants.[15]

'The muezzin had just raised the afternoon call to prayer when Bahá'u'lláh entered the Najíbíyyih Garden . . . There His friends and companions, arriving in successive waves, attained His presence and bade Him, with feelings of profound sorrow, their last farewell. Outstanding among them was the renowned Álúsí, the Muftí of Baghdád, who, with eyes dimmed with tears, execrated the name of Násiri'd-Dín Sháh, whom he deemed to be primarily responsible for so unmerited a banishment. "I have ceased to regard him", he openly asserted, "as Násiri'd-Dín (the helper of the Faith), but consider him rather to be its wrecker." Another distinguished visitor was the governor himself, Námiq Páshá, who, after expressing in the most respectful terms his regret at the developments which had precipitated Bahá'u'lláh's departure, and assuring Him of his readiness to aid Him in any way he could, handed to the officer appointed to accompany Him a written order, commanding the governors of the provinces through which the exiles would be passing to extend to them the utmost consideration. "Whatever you require," he, after profuse apologies, informed Bahá'u'lláh, "you have but to command. We are ready to carry it out." "Extend thy consideration to Our loved ones," was the reply to his insistent and reiterated offers, "and deal with them with kindness" – a request to which he gave his warm and unhesitating assent.'[16]

Once again Bahá'u'lláh had confounded His enemies, who witnessed with bitter remorse the waves of acclamation and love which their machinations had served to arouse in the populace. They were to see yet greater demonstrations of these same, and even deeper, sentiments as the day approached when Bahá'u'lláh would set out in conspicuous majesty and glory to the capital of a mighty empire. Little wonder that Namíq Páshá should confide to Bahá'u'lláh, 'Formerly they insisted on your departure. Now, however, they are even more insistent that you should remain.'[17]

Chapter 11

BAHÁ'U'LLÁH'S DECLARATION OF HIS MISSION

TOWARDS the end of Bahá'u'lláh's sojourn in Iraq, the Bábí community, under the influence of the regenerative and reconstructive measures which He continually poured out upon them, began to emerge once again as an observable Order, characterized by the exalted morals and ethical standards inculcated by the Báb. Throughout Persia, in its major cities and towns, its villages and hamlets, remnants of the battered community, survivors of the fearful holocaust intended to eradicate its very name from Persian soil, were to be found, subdued and leaderless but with the fire which the Báb had kindled in their souls still unquenched. During the difficult days following Bahá'u'lláh's imprisonment and removal from their midst, they had received no support or encouragement from Yaḥyá, who went from place to place in various disguises and pursuing various occupations, in craven fear of an enemy who knew him to be the nominal head of the community. The disastrous undercover activities in which he had engaged when Bahá'u'lláh first arrived in Baghdad, which were a major factor in promoting His retirement to the wilderness of Kurdistan, had very nearly brought about the disintegration of the Bábí community, an outcome which all the fearful butchery and terror unleashed against it by the 'ulamá of Shi'ah Islam could not achieve.

Immediately the news of Bahá'u'lláh's survival and return to Baghdad was heard in Iran the relapsed hopes of the Bábís began to rise again and many of them set out for Baghdad or joined the bands of pilgrims visiting the holy cities in that area. They were able to see for themselves the growing ascendancy of Bahá'u'lláh within and without the community and to recognize the signs of His leadership. Some of them stayed to swell the Bahá'í colony, but many returned to confirm the rumours which had begun to percolate through to Iran of a renascent Bábí community.

'Seven years of uninterrupted, of patient and eminently successful consolidation'[1] wrought such a transformation in the shepherdless community as to render it able to sustain and even anticipate the momentous events about to take place. Following the majestic challenge which He had flung in the face of the assembled 'ulamá, a sense of expectancy began to vibrate throughout the Bábí world. The Báb had made significant allusions to the 'year eighty' (1280 AH, 1863 AD) with reference to 'Him Whom God shall make manifest'. As that historic hour drew near Bahá'u'lláh began to experience, and to communicate progressively to His followers, the approaching manifestation of that mighty force which had invested His being in the Síyáh-Chál. 'The festive, the soul-entrancing odes which He revealed almost every day; the Tablets, replete with hints, which streamed from His pen; the allusions which, in private converse and public discourse, He made to the approaching hour; the exaltation which in moments of joy and sadness alike flooded His soul; the ecstasy which filled His lovers, already enraptured by the multiplying evidences of His rising greatness and glory; the perceptible change noted in His demeanor; and finally, His adoption of the táj (tall felt head-dress), on the day of His departure . . . all proclaimed unmistakably His imminent assumption of the prophetic office and of His open leadership of the community of the Báb's followers.'[2]

Nabíl records the excitement which infused the hearts of

Bahá'u'lláh's companions in the days immediately preceding
the declaration of His mission: 'Many a night would Mírzá
Áqá Ján gather them together in his room, close the door,
light numerous camphorated candles, and chant aloud to them
the newly revealed odes and Tablets in his possession. Wholly
oblivious of this contingent world, completely immersed in
the realms of the spirit, forgetful of the necessity for food,
sleep or drink, they would suddenly discover that night had
become day, and that the sun was approaching its zenith.'[3]

No detailed description of the actual words with which
Bahá'u'lláh clothed His declaration, nor of the specific circumstances in which the 'Great Announcement' was made have
come down to us. We must be grateful to Nabíl for his brief
account of those unimaginably wonderful days, surely unique
in the history of the world: 'Every day, ere the hour of dawn,
the gardeners would pick the roses which lined the four
avenues of the garden, and would pile them in the centre of
the floor of His blessed tent. So great would be the heap that
when His companions gathered to drink their morning tea in
His presence, they would be unable to see each other across
it. All these roses Bahá'u'lláh would, with His own hands,
entrust to those whom He dismissed from His presence every
morning to be delivered, on His behalf, to His Arab and
Persian friends in the city. One night, the ninth night of the
waxing moon, I happened to be one of those who watched
beside His blessed tent. As the hour of midnight approached,
I saw Him issue from His tent, pass by the places where some
of his companions were sleeping, and begin to pace up and
down the moonlit, flower-bordered avenues of the garden. So
loud was the singing of the nightingales on every side that
only those who were near Him could hear distinctly His voice.
He continued to walk until, pausing in the midst of one of
these avenues, He observed: "Consider these nightingales. So
great is their love for these roses, that sleepless from dusk till
dawn, they warble their melodies and commune with burning
passion with the object of their adoration. How then can those

who claim to be afire with the rose-like beauty of the Beloved choose to sleep?" For three successive nights I watched and circled round His blessed tent. Every time I passed by the couch whereon He lay, I would find Him wakeful, and every day, from morn till eventide, I would see Him ceaselessly engaged in conversing with the stream of visitors who kept flowing in from Baghdád. Not once could I discover in the words He spoke any trace of dissimulation.'[4]*

Bahá'u'lláh Himself has testified in innumerable passages to the import of the declaration of His mission. The world-shattering, long-anticipated, most portentous moment in all history had, at last, inevitably arrived. The All-Glorious King of Kings, Lord of Lords, Counsellor, the Prince of Peace, Jesus Christ returned in the glory of the everlasting Father, the Promised One of all ages, anticipated and extolled by the Prophets and Messengers of the past in all the sacred scriptures, had ascended His throne. The Day of God had come.

Rejoice with exceeding gladness, O people of Bahá, as ye call to remembrance the Day of supreme felicity, the Day whereon the Tongue of the Ancient of Days hath spoken, as He departed from His House, proceeding to the Spot from which He shed upon the whole of creation the splendours of His name, the All-Merciful.

This is the Day whereon the unseen world crieth out: 'Great is thy blessedness, O earth, for thou hast been made the foot-stool of thy God, and been chosen as the seat of His mighty throne.'

Arise, and proclaim unto the entire creation the tidings that He Who is the All-Merciful hath directed His steps towards the Riḍván and entered it. Guide, then, the people unto the garden of delight which God hath made the Throne of His Paradise.

The Revelation which, from time immemorial, hath been acclaimed as the Purpose and Promise of all the Prophets of God, and the most cherished Desire of His Messengers, hath now, by virtue of the pervasive Will of the Almighty and at His irresistible bidding, been

---

* In certain sects of Islam it is permissible for a believer under duress to deny his Faith; this is referred to as 'dissimulation'.

revealed unto men. The advent of such a Revelation hath been heralded in all the sacred Scriptures. Behold how, notwithstanding such an announcement, mankind hath strayed from its path and shut out itself from its glory.

Verily I say, this is the Day in which mankind can behold the Face, and hear the Voice, of the Promised One. The Call of God hath been raised, and the light of His countenance hath been lifted up upon men. It behoveth every man to blot out the trace of every idle word from the tablet of his heart, and to gaze, with an open and unbiased mind, on the signs of His Revelation, the proofs of His Mission, and the tokens of His glory.

Great indeed is this Day! The allusions made to it in all the sacred Scriptures as the Day of God attest its greatness. The soul of every Prophet of God, of every Divine Messenger, hath thirsted for this wondrous Day. All the divers kindreds of the earth have, likewise, yearned to attain it. No sooner, however, had the Day Star of His Revelation manifested itself in the heaven of God's Will, than all, except those whom the Almighty was pleased to guide, were found dumbfounded and heedless.

This is the Day in which God's most excellent favours have been poured out upon men, the Day in which His most mighty grace hath been infused into all created things. It is incumbent upon all the peoples of the world to reconcile their differences, and, with perfect unity and peace, abide beneath the shadow of the Tree of His care and loving-kindness. It behoveth them to cleave to whatsover will, in this Day, be conducive to the exaltation of their stations, and to the promotion of their best interests. Happy are those whom the all-glorious Pen was moved to remember, and blessed are those men whose names, by virtue of Our inscrutable decree, We have preferred to conceal.

Verily this is that Most Great Beauty, foretold in the Books of the Messengers, through Whom truth shall be distinguished from error and the wisdom of every command shall be tested. Verily He is the Tree of Life that bringeth forth the fruits of God, the Exalted, the Powerful, the Great. [5]

Yet this mighty event was but a prelude to the greater,

more powerful and widespread proclamation of His mission which He would make from Adrianople and the 'Most Great Prison' of 'Akká during the third and fourth stages of His exile, when He would address the kings and rulers of the world, its secular and religious hierarchies, its communities, its legislatures, philosophers and wise men and the people.

On the ninth day of the Riḍván Festival Bahá'u'lláh's family joined Him in the garden, and final preparation was made for the caravan to set out on its thousand-mile journey. The twelfth, the final day of that Festival witnessed scenes of such tumultuous enthusiasm and uninhibited emotion as transcended the popular demonstrations which had taken place when Bahá'u'lláh left His house in Baghdad on the other side of the river.

The despair of the Bábís from the moment they learned of Bahá'u'lláh's impending departure was in no way assuaged by His declaration, which was known only to those few who were in the garden at the time and who would go with Him to Turkey. The larger community was torn with the pain of separation; so great was their sorrow that even the few who would accompany their Lord wept with them. The great news was not widely disseminated at that time. Though they knew Bahá'u'lláh as their leader, spiritual guide and protector, they could not, without knowledge of His declaration, foresee that the Bábí community, as intended by its Founder, the glorious Báb, would effloresce into the Bahá'í World Community, ere long to establish the seat of its spiritual and administrative institutions on God's Holy Mountain, and to proclaim its message of love and justice and unity in every inhabited part of the earth.

Towards late afternoon of the twelfth day of Riḍván, when all was ready, Bahá'u'lláh was seen to mount His steed. At that moment, all chroniclers agree, cries of unbearable distress, of heartrending sorrow, arose from the vast crowd. Time and again calls of 'Alláh-u-Akbar' (God is most great) rang out from every side. 'Mounted on His steed, a red roan stallion of the finest breed, the best His lovers could purchase for Him, and leaving behind Him a bowing multitude of fervent admirers, He rode forth on the first stage of a journey that was to carry Him to the city of Constantinople' is Shoghi Effendi's noble evocation of that memorable scene. The ever-reliable Nabíl, who was present throughout those days, recounts, 'Numerous were the heads which, on every side, bowed to the dust at the feet of His horse, and kissed its hoofs, and countless were those who pressed forward to embrace His stirrups.'[6]

Bahá'u'lláh Himself testified,

He [God] it was Who enabled Me to depart out of the city [Baghdad] clothed with such majesty as none, except the denier and the malicious, can fail to acknowledge.[7]

Chapter 12

BY CARAVAN TO CONSTANTINOPLE

IN in his monumental work,* H. M. Balyuzi describes Bahá'u'lláh's journey from Baghdad to Constantinople as 'The March of the King of Glory', and he relates the circumstances in which the same honour accorded Him by the sorrowing multitudes as He left their city continued to be showered upon Him and His retinue as they traversed the plains and foothills, the deserts and stony mountain passes, the uplands, woods and pastures of Anatolia. For the members of that immortal caravan it was a period of uninterrupted happiness, the longest (four months less ten days) in the entire course of Bahá'u'lláh's tragedy-laden, star-studded, sacrificial ministry stretching from that day in 1844 when He had enlisted as one of the earliest followers of the Báb to His death in 1892, a prisoner and an exile far from His native home. For Bahá'u'lláh Himself it was but the lull before the storm, as He well knew and had indicated in the *Tablet of the Holy Mariner*.

To this modern generation it is difficult to imagine such a journey as we are now contemplating. In that unpolluted part of the world, there were, at that time, no railways, no aeroplanes, no motor cars, no paved roads, no electricity, no telephones; muscle power, animal or human, was the sole

---

* *Bahá'u'lláh, The King of Glory.*

source of energy. Those caravans on 'the golden road to Samarkand' or even the covered wagons of the great American plains or the African veldt have long since entered the world of romance, and the bustle and excitement and logistical skill involved in mobilizing a caravan of fifty mules, a few howdahs, less than a hundred people and a dozen soldiers is unlikely to be overestimated by a generation which can transport half a million militia with their equipment halfway round the world in a couple of weeks. Yet it is less than a hundred and thirty years since this caravan, whose story is destined to be told and retold for countless centuries, set out on its thousand-mile journey.

It was springtime and the Governor of Baghdad himself ensured that the appointments of the train should be in keeping with the respectful terms of the invitation from the Grand Vizier. Bahá'u'lláh's devoted admirer, he had needed no urging to inform every headman, mufti, mayor or person in authority in all the towns and villages along the route, of the honour conferred upon them by the passing of so exalted a Person through their domains. He had further provided the officer of the escort with a letter requiring these same authorities to supply the caravan with whatever necessities it might require. Bahá'u'lláh, however, forbade the use of this exaction and insisted that everything obtained from the local communities should be paid for.

With such good will, and with the acclamation of the population of Baghdad still ringing in their ears and the perfume of the roses from the Garden of Riḍván still fragrant in their nostrils, the beatified members of that exalted company, the companions of the Lord of Hosts, the Promised One of all ages, He Whom God *had* made manifest, began their royal progress.

Nabíl records the 'unanimous testimony' of the people they met throughout that journey who declared that they had never seen anyone travel in such state. Námiq Páshá's written order was fully implemented and Bahá'u'lláh was accorded, as

Shoghi Effendi noted, 'an enthusiastic reception by the válís, the mutisarrifs, the qá'im-maqáms, the mudírs, the shaykhs, the muftís and qadís, the government officials and notables belonging to the districts through which He passed.'[1]

Balyuzi records that 'while on the move' Bahá'u'lláh would generally ride in a howdah, but when approaching a town or village He would mount His horse to meet the dignitaries who came out to welcome Him.

When He neared a town or settlement it was usual for a delegation of the notables to welcome Him, escort Him through its main thoroughfares, and accompany Him some distance along the onward journey. At places where they rested, festivities would be held in His honour, food would be prepared and joyfully presented for His acceptance, and everything which could contribute to His comfort was eagerly undertaken.

At one of the large towns on the way, Márdín, a situation arose which provides us with a wonderful example of Bahá'u'lláh's high sense of justice, a principle greatly stressed in His revelation. The caravan had encamped for the night at a small village below the town. Hasan Balyuzi takes up the story. 'There, during the night, two mules, belonging to an Arab travelling with the caravan, were stolen. The owner was beside himself with grief. Bahá'u'lláh asked the official who accompanied the caravan to try and find the missing animals. Other officials were called in, but no animal was forthcoming. As the caravan was on the point of departing, the poor Arab went crying to Bahá'u'lláh. "You are leaving," he moaned, "and I shall never get back my beasts." Bahá'u'lláh immediately called off the resumption of the journey. "We will go to Firdaws [a nearby estate] and stay there", He said, "until this man's mules are found and restored to him."

'. . . The Mutasarrif threatened the headman of the village, where the mules had been stolen, with imprisonment if the animals were not found. The headman offered a sum of money in lieu of the mules. But Bahá'u'lláh insisted that the Arab was entitled to have his beasts restored to him. On the second day the headman came with a promissory note guaranteed by higher officials, offering to pay 60 pounds within a month, the value of the two mules. But Bahá'u'lláh refused this offer too. Then the headman realized that the game was up, sent for the animals and gave them to their distraught owner. People were amazed, for such a thing had never happened before. No stolen property had ever been retrieved, nor restitution made to the rightful owner. Áqá Ḥusayn-i-Áshchí, in his reminiscences some four decades later, recalled that various officials went to Bahá'u'lláh to speak of the part they had played in retrieving the beasts and received suitable rewards. The Mutaṣarrif was given a costly cashmere shawl, the Muftí an illuminated copy of the Qur'án, the head of the horsemen a sword with bejewelled scabbard.

'The purpose of the halt at Firdaws achieved, Bahá'u'lláh ordered the resumption of the journey on the third day. And what was seen then was also an event of rare splendour. The road lay through the main street of the city of Márdín. Government cavalry with flags flying and drums beating preceded the caravan; then came the caravan escorted by the Mutaṣarrif himself with other high officials and notables. And the whole town had come out, thronging the streets to hail and see the passage of the caravan. It was a slow descent from the mountain-top, and then Bahá'u'lláh bade farewell to the escort and told the men to go back to their town; while the caravan went on its way, moving all day long through copses and over lush meadows, until a halt was called at the end of the day, in a verdant spot beside running water.'[2]

As apparent from the above incident, other travellers would join the caravan from time to time, either for protection or companionship or both. One such was Mírzá Yaḥyá, who joined at Mosul and remained in the company of the exiles until the final banishment, when he was sent to Cyprus. Mosul was sufficiently far from the Persian border to enable him to come out of hiding, but he did not disclose his identity and since only two or three members of the company knew him, he was regarded by most of them as a travelling Jew.

Although the actual travelling was extremely tiring — according to 'Abdu'l-Bahá they often covered, by day or night, a distance of twenty-five to thirty miles, resting for two days or more at a time — their journey was enlivened by a great variety of incidents, not always unfortunate or critical, which together with the beauty, often spectacular, of the scenery and the many famous historical associations of the region, provided a constant interest to their days. Superimposed on all this was the overwhelming sense of the unique character of their mission, the exaltation, which still possessed them, of those ineffable days in the Garden of Riḍván when the King of kings had permitted the veil which concealed His glory to be momentarily drawn aside, the splendour of their progress as they conducted Him along His way, all of which invested that immortal company with a supernal joy and exultation whose memory will remain undimmed through ages to come.

'Abdu'l-Bahá, at that time barely twenty years old — although the responsibilities which He had shouldered in Baghdad, as He Himself testified, had aged Him — recounted how He and another youth, one who had so far lived a life of ease and pleasure in Persia, measured out the miles together. 'He was a close companion of mine on that journey. There were nights when we would walk, one to either side of the howdah of Bahá'u'lláh, and the joy we had defies description. Some of those nights he would sing poems; among them he would chant the odes of Ḥáfiẓ, like the one that begins "Come let us scatter these roses . . ."' [3]

On one occasion two mules were washed away by the rushing waters of one of the great rivers of the region. At Arbil they camped on the site of one of Alexander's great victories over the Persians in 331 BC. Further on, the scene was that of the great battle a thousand years later in which the fate of the Umayyads was finally decided.

At Karkúk the river, swiftly running and cold, was crossed

by a high bridge. An athlete of the town dived from the bridge, a feat which so pleased Bahá'u'lláh that He received the man and gave him some money.

Áqá Ridá* got lost one night. The caravan had set out in pitch darkness and a high wind, and as he walked along, sleeping intermittently, he noticed that the mule carrying Bahá'u'lláh's howdah had stopped, while some slight repair was being made. The mule's attendant had sat down, so Áqá Ridá did likewise and promptly fell asleep. He awoke five hours later to find the caravan had gone on without him. Fortunately it stopped at dawn for the morning prayers and Áqá Ridá was able to catch up with it, just as Mírzá Músá was about to send out men to look for him.

Whenever the departure of the caravan from a resting place was delayed, Bahá'u'lláh instructed His companions to cultivate the land and sow seeds so that the beneficial effect of their visit would be visibly marked.

At most resting places the local officials would place guards round the camp as a protection against highwaymen. On the one occasion when the members of the caravan had to do this, they arranged themselves in groups. One group chanted aloud, 'Whose is the dominion?' and another would answer, 'God's, the All-Powerful, the All-Mighty.'

Who would not have joined that heavenly caravan?

They reached Samsun, the port on the Black Sea, whence they were taken by steamer to Constantinople. They had to wait eight days for the ship, during which time the Chief Inspector of the entire province through which they had just passed called on Bahá'u'lláh and was entertained by Him at luncheon. He and the pashas of the place showed Him the greatest respect. He disembarked at Constantinople on August

* A devout and trusted member of the retinue, Áqá Ridá said that he wrote his own account of those stirring days at the request of Nabíl, who sought eyewitness accounts of things which he, himself, had not seen. See Balyuzi, *Bahá'u'lláh, The King of Glory.*

6th, 1863. Thus ended 'the march of the King of Glory' and opened the grimmest, most tragic, most glorious, most momentous epoch of His entire ministry.

Chapter 13

THE THIRD BANISHMENT

BAHÁ'U'LLÁH was courteously received on arrival at Constantinople by the government official designated for that duty, who brought the whole party to his own house. This was immediately seen to be too small for so many people and within a month they were moved to a more palatial residence which gave them ample accommodation, as well as its own Turkish bath and vast garden.

The Persian ambassador to the Sublime Porte had been constantly urged by his masters to provoke and foster the hostility of the Turkish authorities against Bahá'u'lláh. He was assiduous in that duty and after some years of persistent misrepresentation and calumniation had won the support of the Sultan's two most powerful ministers, the Grand Vizier and the Foreign Minister. Indeed it was the influence of these two, 'Alí Páshá and Fu'ád Páshá respectively, which had finally induced the Sultan, who for two years had refused the constant requests of the Persian government, to so far accede to their persistent pressure as to invite Bahá'u'lláh to his capital.

Bahá'u'lláh's implacable enemies in the Persian government were far from satisfied with the courteous tone and intent of the Sultan's invitation to Him. They had hoped for some punitive measure which would either deliver Him into their hands or remove Him to some far corner of the Turkish empire where He could be left to languish in ignominious obscurity. His triumphal tour from Baghdad to the capital, where He continued to receive the respect and marks of attention normally reserved for highly-honoured guests, inflamed their malicious hatred, which was to pursue Him for the rest of His days. Even after His passing, their hatred would be visited upon the ever-growing community of His followers, until their unbridled cruelty in recurrent outbursts of terror would be brought to the attention of the highest tribunal which mankind has yet devised, thereby proclaiming to the nations and international agencies of the world, that very Message which it was their intention to eradicate from human memory.

The day after Bahá'u'lláh's arrival in Constantinople an envoy from the Persian embassy called on Him to present the compliments of the ambassador and to say that circumstances prevented him from coming in person and he must forego the pleasure of a visit. Bahá'u'lláh made no comment and did not return the deputy's call.

The corruption which pervaded the Sultan's court, no less than it did the Persian nobility, was nowhere more clearly displayed than in the conduct of those royal drones and Persians of high degree who on their arrival at the Sublime Porte immediately began 'to solicit at every door such allowances and gifts as they might obtain'. It was quickly intimated to Bahá'u'lláh that the diplomatic niceties would be observed were He to call on the Foreign Minister – after a prescribed delay of three days – and seek through him an interview with the Grand Vizier, who would convey His request for an audience to the Sultan. Bahá'u'lláh responded to these overtures by saying that He had no favour to solicit, no project to further, and since He had come to the capital by invitation of the Ottoman government it was for them to approach Him if they had anything to convey to Him.

This independent and noble stance taken by Bahá'u'lláh was seized upon by the Persian ambassador as an opportunity to strike at Him again. Ignoring the fact that Bahá'u'lláh had protected Himself and His companions against the enmity of the Persian authorities by obtaining Turkish citizenship, he resented Bahá'u'lláh's refusal to present Himself at the Persian embassy and used all the opportunities of his office to initiate a campaign of misrepresentation, portraying Bahá'u'lláh as an arrogant, proud and high-handed person opposed to all authority, whose ambition was the real source of all the trouble between Himself and the Persian government. These calumnies were as meat and drink to those self-seeking intriguers who flooded the ranks of government, all of whom knew themselves to be impugned by Bahá'u'lláh's upright conduct. 'Abdu'l-'Azíz, the Sultan, was unable to resist the pressure mounted by his two most trusted ministers, the envoy of a friendly power, and the general attitude of the court, and the desired edict was issued.

Suddenly, with no warning, all was changed for the exiles. A relative of the Grand Vizier was sent to inform Bahá'u'lláh of the firmán which decreed the instant banishment of Himself and all His company to one of the most remote and unattractive parts of the empire, the ancient and decrepit city of Adrianople on the northernmost border of Turkey-in-Europe. Shoghi Effendi wrote in *God Passes By** that this was 'an edict which evinced a virtual coalition of the Turkish and Persian imperial governments against a common adversary, and which in the end brought such tragic consequences upon the Sultanate, the Caliphate and the Qájár dynasty'.†

Bahá'u'lláh's anger was enkindled by this manifestly unjust action, and His immediate intention was to refuse to comply, whatever the consequences. In this He was supported by the staunch members of His family and followers. But then Mírzá Yaḥyá, poltroon as ever, pleaded the cause of the wives and children. Bahá'u'lláh replied that they could all be cared for by the foreign envoys in the city. These, with many other highly-placed persons, had come to appreciate, even in the short time of His stay among them, that exaltation and

---

* All the quotations in this chapter are from *God Passes By*, chapter 9, pp. 158–61.
† See Chapter 14, pp. 110–12, 118.

radiance which had always charmed the well-intentioned and provoked the malicious. However, Bahá'u'lláh perceived the danger of a rift in the community and agreed to accept the edict. But he commented that if they had stood firm, even to the point of martyrdom, the event would have redounded to the fame of the Cause of God, and possibly nothing would have happened to them anyway.

Once more the little band of exiles with their belongings mounted the wagons, the mules and the oxcarts and set out on another banishment. But this time it was no march of glory, but one of bitter suffering, reminiscent of the early stages of that first journey over the snow-covered mountains of western Persia. This was a shorter journey, occupying twelve days over a flat countryside gripped in a cold of such intensity that 'nonagenarians could not recall its like'. Bahá'u'lláh testifies, 'Neither My family, nor those who accompanied Me had the necessary raiment to protect them from the cold in that freezing weather.' They arrived in Adrianople, now called Edirne, on December 12th, 1863 and remained there for four years.

Bahá'u'lláh's arrival in Constantinople and subsequent residence in Adrianople marks the first occasion for which there is any authentic record of a Manifestation of God setting foot on European soil.*

Among His many writings during His brief stay in the Turkish capital, two stand out as being of great significance in the vast ocean of His revelation; one brief, the other of considerable length. To the Persian ambassador, His relentless enemy and the focal point of all the intrigues and opposition at the heart of the Ottoman empire which had brought about His second and third exiles, Bahá'u'lláh wrote on the eve of the journey to Adrianople:

What did it profit thee, and such as are like thee, to slay, year after

---

* Geoffrey Ashe and others have made great play about a supposed visit of Jesus, when a boy, to Glastonbury in south-west England. The legend was the inspiration of Blake's famous hymn *Jerusalem*: 'And did those feet in ancient time walk upon England's mountains green . . .'

year, so many of the oppressed, and to inflict upon them manifold
afflictions, when they have increased a hundredfold, and ye find
yourselves in complete bewilderment, knowing not how to relieve
your minds of this oppressive thought . . . His Cause transcends
any and every plan ye devise. Know this much: Were all the
governments on earth to unite and take My life and the lives of all
who bear this Name, this Divine Fire would never be quenched.
His Cause will rather encompass all the kings of the earth, nay all
that hath been created from water and clay . . . Whatever may yet
befall Us, great shall be our gain, and manifest the loss wherewith
they shall be afflicted.

This powerful statement was preceded by a lengthy letter
to 'Alí Páshá, the Grand Vizier, written to him on the same
day that his messenger delivered the Sultan's edict. We have
no copy of that letter, but Nabíl, who was present when it was
revealed and probably transcribed it, says that it 'was of
considerable length, opened with words directed to the
sovereign himself, severely censured his ministers, exposed
their immaturity and incompetence, and included passages in
which the ministers themselves were addressed, in which they
were boldly challenged, and sternly admonished not to pride
themselves on their wordly possessions, nor foolishly seek the
riches of which time would inexorably rob them'.

Shamsí Big, the official appointed to act as host to the
exiles, was handed this letter in a sealed envelope and
instructed by Bahá'u'lláh to deliver it to the Grand Vizier
himself and to say that it was sent down from God. Shamsí
Big reported later to Mírzá Músá, 'I know not what that letter
contained for no sooner had the Grand Vizier perused it than
he turned the colour of a corpse, and remarked: "It is as if the
King of kings were issuing his behest to his humblest vassal
king and regulating his conduct." So grievous was his condition
that I backed out of his presence.'

Bahá'u'lláh commented:

Whatever action the ministers of the Sultán took against Us, after
having become acquainted with its contents, cannot be regarded as

unjustifiable. The acts they committed before its perusal, however, can have no justification.

The revelation and delivery of this Tablet, Shoghi Effendi hails as the initiation of the great proclamation of His Message which Bahá'u'lláh was about to make from Adrianople to the kings and religious leaders of the world. 'Abdu'l-'Azíz, 'the self-styled vicar of the Prophet of Islám and the absolute ruler of a mighty empire . . . was the first among the sovereigns of the world to receive the Divine Summons, and the first among Oriental monarchs to sustain the impact of God's retributive justice'.

Chapter 14

THE PROCLAMATION TO THE KINGS AND RELIGIOUS LEADERS

BAHÁ'U'LLÁH'S sojourn in Adrianople* was the mid-point of His ministry and lasted four years and eight months. It was there that the sun of His revelation rose to its zenith, manifest in the mounting respect shown to Him by local officials from the governor down, by the entire diplomatic corps – still numerous in that ancient capital – by the religious communities of various faiths, and by the initiation of that huge proclamation of His mission to the kings and rulers and ecclesiastical leaders of the world which is so outstanding a feature of His ministry. And it was there that the greatest crisis ever to afflict His Faith was sustained and surmounted. These two events will forever distinguish the period of banishment in Adrianople.

It is hard to realize that a mere twenty years had elapsed since that world-shattering, apocalyptic event – the declaration of the Báb – had taken place in Shiraz; tumultuous years filled with great events of immense portent to the unfoldment of the new age which had dawned upon the world's horizon and of which the world was as yet unaware. The entire 'Episode

---

* It was an important city in ancient times. It was rebuilt by the Roman Emperor Hadrian and named after him. At one time it was the capital of the Turkish empire. It is now called Edirne.

of the Báb' with all its bestial horror, magnificent heroism, and sublime sacrifice adorned the first years of that period, and was immediately succeeded by an event of unsurpassed significance in the entire history of mankind – the investiture of Bahá'u'lláh with His divine station and mission as He lay in chains in the Síyáh-Chál. In swift succession there followed His banishment to Baghdad, His retirement to Sulaymáníyyih, the decline of the Bábí community, His return and the dramatic regeneration of that tragic people, the rapid growth of His ascendancy in and beyond Baghdad attaining such a peak of grandeur as to invoke the attention of the two most autocratic and powerful despots of the age – the Shah and the Sultan – the unanswerable challenge which He issued to the assembled leaders of Shi'ah Islam, the majesty of His journey into a second exile and the stroke of venomous hatred which decreed His third banishment. All these events centred around that one lonely Figure, an Exile despoiled of all His great possessions, deposed from His high station among men, reduced to the utter abasement of a prisoner in chains, yet chosen by God to be the Redeemer of mankind, empowered to effect the divine alchemy of transforming 'satanic strength into heavenly power' and to lay the foundation of God's own kingdom on this earth on 'an enduring foundation' which 'storms of human strife are powerless to undermine' or 'men's fanciful theories' to damage.

Until and for some time after He left Baghdad Bahá'u'lláh was considered to be a Bábí. His declaration in the Garden of Ridván was made only to those few who were present and was not a public announcement. To some it was a confirmation of what they had already recognized, while to others it was the fulfilment of their hopes. It was not communicated to any outside the Bábí community, not even to the Governor and those notables who were so greatly devoted to Him. His writings during the Baghdad period included, in addition to the great number of odes and meditations which flowed from His pen in Kurdistan, some of the great works which form the basis of His revelation, the *Kitáb-i-Íqán (Book of Certitude)*, the *Hidden Words* and the *Seven Valleys*, but in none of them did He disclose the mission which had been entrusted to Him in the Síyáh-<u>Ch</u>ál.

Now in Adrianople, Bahá'u'lláh openly assumed the mantle of His Prophethood and began a mighty proclamation of His advent and of His mission, not only to the kings and rulers and religious leaders of the world, but to mankind in general and their elected representatives. Never in the history of the world had the Manifestation of God made so widespread, specific and unambiguous a statement of His mission.

Napoleon III, the Czar, Queen Victoria, the Pope, the Sultan and the Shah were sent individual letters, and 'Abdu'l-'Azíz, the Sultan, was further addressed in a general letter to 'the Kings of the earth'. The Emperors of Austria and of Germany, the 'Rulers of America and the Presidents of the Republics therein', the world's religious leaders and particularly those of Christianity and Islam, were addressed in the *Kitáb-i-Aqdas*, the Most Holy Book of the Bahá'í revelation, and in innumerable Tablets the peoples of the world and their elected representatives were summoned to service in this day of God.

The opening note of that great summons was sounded from Constantinople by the delivery of that condemnatory and challenging Tablet to Sultán 'Abdu'l-'Azíz described in the preceding chapter. That tyrannical despot was addressed again in the early passages of the mighty *Súriy-i-Mulúk (Tablet to the Kings)* and sent two verbal messages in the course of Bahá'u'lláh's journey to His final place of banishment* in the Holy Land.

The *Súriy-i-Mulúk* is among the weightiest and most majestic of Bahá'u'lláh's works. In it He addresses the 'entire company of the monarchs of East and West [and specifically Sultán 'Abdu'l-'Azíz], the kings of Christendom, the French and Persian ambassadors accredited to the Sublime Porte, the Muslim ecclesiastical leaders in Constantinople, its wise men

---

* From Baghdad to Constantinople, thence to Adrianople, and finally to 'Akká.

and inhabitants, the people of Persia and the philosophers of the world'.[1]

From this weighty Tablet we quote the following:*

O Kings of the earth! He Who is the sovereign Lord of all is come. The Kingdom is God's, the omnipotent Protector, the Self-Subsisting. Worship none but God, and, with radiant hearts, lift up your faces unto your Lord, the Lord of all names. This is a Revelation to which whatever ye possess can never be compared, could ye but know it. We see you rejoicing in that which ye have amassed for others, and shutting out yourselves from the worlds which naught except My Guarded Tablet can reckon. The treasures ye have laid up have drawn you far away from your ultimate objective. This ill beseemeth you, could ye but understand it. Wash your hearts from all earthly defilements, and hasten to enter the Kingdom of your Lord, the Creator of earth and heaven, Who caused the world to tremble, and all its peoples to wail, except them that have renounced all things and clung to that which the Hidden Tablet hath ordained . . .

By the righteousness of God! It is not Our wish to lay hands on your kingdoms. Our mission is to seize and possess the hearts of men. Upon them the eyes of Bahá are fastened. To this testifieth the Kingdom of Names, could ye but comprehend it.

Beware not to deal unjustly with any one that appealeth to you, and entereth beneath your shadow. Walk ye in the fear of God, and be ye of them that lead a godly life. Rest not on your power, your armies, and treasures. Put your whole trust and confidence in God, Who hath created you, and seek ye His help in all your affairs. Succour cometh from Him alone. He succoureth whom He willeth with the hosts of the heavens and of the earth.

Know ye that the poor are the trust of God in your midst. Watch that ye betray not His trust, that ye deal not unjustly with them and that ye walk not in the ways of the treacherous. Ye will most certainly be called upon to answer for His trust on the day when the Balance of Justice shall be set, the day when unto every one

---

* Most of the following passages can be found in the collection of Bahá'u'lláh's Tablets to the kings and rulers entitled *The Proclamation of Bahá'u'lláh*. Haifa: Bahá'í World Centre, 1967. Those which cannot are indicated.

shall be rendered his due, when the doings of all men, be they rich or poor, shall be weighed.

If ye pay no heed unto the counsels which, in peerless and unequivocal language, We have revealed in this Tablet, Divine chastisement shall assail you from every direction, and the sentence of His justice shall be pronounced against you. On that day ye shall have no power to resist Him, and shall recognize your own impotence. Have mercy on yourselves and on those beneath you, and judge ye between them according to the precepts prescribed by God in His most holy and exalted Tablet, a Tablet wherein He hath assigned to each and every thing its settled measure, in which He hath given, with distinctness, an explanation of all things, and which is in itself a monition unto them that believe in Him.

Examine Our Cause, inquire into the things that have befallen Us, and decide justly between Us and Our enemies, and be ye of them that act equitably towards their neighbours. If ye stay not the hand of the oppressor, if ye fail to safeguard the rights of the down-trodden, what right have ye then to vaunt yourselves among men? What is it of which ye can rightly boast? Is it on your food and your drink that ye pride yourselves, on the riches ye lay up in your treasuries, on the diversity and the cost of the ornaments with which ye deck yourselves? . . .

O Kings of the earth! We see you increasing every year your expenditures, and laying the burden thereof on your subjects. This, verily, is wholly and grossly unjust. Fear the sighs and tears of this Wronged One, and lay not excessive burdens on your peoples. Do not rob them to rear palaces for yourselves; nay rather- choose for them that which ye choose for yourselves. Thus We unfold to your eyes that which profiteth you, if ye but perceive. Your people are your treasures. Beware lest your rule violate the commandments of God, and ye deliver your wards to the hands of the robber. By them ye rule, by their means ye subsist, by their aid ye conquer. Yet, how disdainfully ye look upon them! How strange, how very strange!

Now that ye have refused the Most Great Peace, hold ye fast unto this, the Lesser Peace, that haply ye may in some degree better your own condition and that of your dependents.

O Rulers of the earth! Be reconciled among yourselves, that ye may need no more armaments save in a measure to safeguard your territories and dominions. Beware lest ye disregard the counsel of the All-Knowing, the Faithful.

Be united, O Kings of the earth, for thereby will the tempest of discord be stilled amongst you, and your people find rest, if ye be of them that comprehend. Should any one among you take up arms against another, rise ye all against him, for this is naught but manifest justice.

To the Sultan Bahá'u'lláh wrote:

Hearken, O King, to the speech of Him that speaketh the truth, Him that doth not ask thee to recompense Him with the things God hath chosen to bestow upon thee, Him Who unerringly treadeth the straight Path. He it is Who summoneth thee unto God, thy Lord, Who showeth thee the right course, the way that leadeth to true felicity, that haply thou mayest be of them with whom it shall be well.

Beware, O King, that thou gather not around thee such ministers as follow the desires of a corrupt inclination, as have cast behind their backs that which hath been committed into their hands and manifestly betrayed their trust. Be bounteous to others as God hath been bounteous to thee, and abandon not the interests of thy people to the mercy of such ministers as these. Lay not aside the fear of God, and be thou of them that act uprightly. Gather around thee those ministers from whom thou canst perceive the fragrance of faith and of justice, and take thou counsel with them, and choose whatever is best in thy sight, and be of them that act generously

. . .

Overstep not the bounds of moderation, and deal justly with them that serve thee. Bestow upon them according to their needs and not to the extent that will enable them to lay up riches for themselves, to deck their persons, to embellish their homes, to acquire the things that are of no benefit unto them, and to be numbered with the extravagant. Deal with them with undeviating justice, so that none among them may either suffer want, or be pampered with luxuries. This is but manifest justice.

Allow not the abject to rule over and dominate them who are noble and worthy of honour, and suffer not the high-minded to be at the mercy of the contemptible and worthless, for this is what We observed upon our arrival in the City [Constantinople], and to it

We bear witness. We found among its inhabitants some who were possessed of an affluent fortune and lived in the midst of excessive riches, whilst others were in dire want and abject poverty. This ill beseemeth thy sovereignty, and is unworthy of thy rank.

Let My counsel be acceptable to thee, and strive thou to rule with equity among men, that God may exalt thy name and spread abroad the fame of thy justice in all the world. Beware lest thou aggrandize thy ministers at the expense of thy subjects. Fear the sighs of the poor and of the upright in heart who, at every break of day, bewail their plight, and be unto them a benignant sovereign. They, verily, are thy treasures on earth. It behoveth thee, therefore, to safeguard thy treasures from the assaults of them who wish to rob thee. Inquire into their affairs, and ascertain, every year, nay every month, their condition, and be not of them that are careless of their duty.

Sultán 'Abdu'l-'Azíz obviously did not hearken to these wise counsels. After he had issued the decree of Bahá'u'lláh's fourth banishment a further message was sent to him, verbally, through the Turkish officer designated to accompany the exiles from Adrianople to their port of embarkation for 'Akká. At Gallipoli Bahá'u'lláh addressed this officer, Ḥasan Effendi:

Tell the king that this territory will pass out of his hands, and his affairs will be thrown into confusion. Not I speak these words but God . . .[2]

In the *Súriy-i-Ra'ís*, revealed as He left Adrianople, Bahá'u'lláh addressed the Grand Vizier, severely reprimanding him and foretelling his downfall and asserting that His revelation would 'erelong encompass the earth and all that dwell therein'. He continued

The Land of Mystery [Adrianople] and what is beside it . . . shall pass out of the hands of the king, and commotions shall appear, and the voice of lamentation shall be raised, and the evidences of mischief shall be revealed on all sides . . . conditions shall wax so grievous that the very sands on the desolate hills will moan, and the trees on the mountain will weep, and blood will flow out of all things. Then will thou behold the people in sore distress.[3]

It all came about as Bahá'u'lláh foretold. 'Alí Páshá fell from grace and sank into oblivion; the Sultan in one fell swoop lost both his throne and his life; a disastrous war with Russia ensued when Adrianople was occupied. There was great suffering and blood did indeed flow out of all things. The mighty Ottoman Empire never recovered from this disastrous blow and was finally dismembered during World War I after which Kemal Páshá established a new régime in Turkey.

At the time of Bahá'u'lláh's proclamation, the kings and ecclesiastical leaders exercised nearly absolute authority over the generality of mankind. The 'pomp and circumstance' of the European monarchs — as late as the first world war the Kaiser was still referred to as the All-Highest — the unrestrained autocracy of most Asiatic rulers, was paralleled by the complete domination exercised by the ecclesiastical hierarchies of the ancient religions. Kings and priests controlled the political and religious life of the masses. Little wonder that it was to them that Bahá'u'lláh directed the full weight of His divine summons, to them conveyed the wise counsels, unfolded the worldwide vision and described the practical activities by which they could bring great benefit and happiness to all humanity.

Napoleon III, the most ambitious, resplendent and powerful monarch of the time, was twice addressed by Bahá'u'lláh. The first Tablet, sent from Adrianople through a French diplomat, announced to the emperor the new Revelation from God.

This is, truly, that which the Spirit of God [Jesus Christ] hath announced, when He came with truth unto you . . .

Bahá'u'lláh then praises the emperor:

Two statements graciously uttered by the king of the age have reached the ears of these wronged ones. These pronouncements are, in truth, the king of all pronouncements, the like of which have never been heard from any sovereign. The first was the answer given the Russian government when it inquired why the war [Crimean] was waged against it. Thou didst reply: 'The cry of the oppressed who, without guilt or blame, were drowned in the Black Sea wakened me at dawn. Wherefore, I took up arms against thee.' These oppressed ones, however, have suffered a greater wrong, and are in greater distress. Whereas the trials inflicted upon those people lasted but one day, the troubles borne by these servants have continued for twenty and five years, every moment of which has held for us a grievous affliction. The other weighty statement, which was indeed a wondrous statement manifested to the world, was this: 'Ours is the responsibility to avenge the oppressed and succor the helpless.' The fame of the Emperor's justice and fairness hath brought hope to a great many souls. It beseemeth the king of the age to inquire into the condition of such as have been wronged, and it behooveth him to extend his care to the weak. Verily, there hath not been, nor is there now, on earth any one as oppressed as we are, or as helpless as these wanderers.[4]

The emperor is then urged,

Arise thou to serve God and help His Cause. He, verily, will assist thee with the hosts of the seen and unseen, and will set thee king over all that whereon the sun riseth. Thy Lord, in truth, is the All-Powerful, the Almighty.

The breezes of the Most Merciful have passed over all created things; happy the man that hath discovered their fragrance, and set himself towards them with a sound heart. Attire thy temple with the ornament of My Name, and thy tongue with remembrance of Me, and thine heart with love for Me, the Almighty, the Most High. We have desired for thee naught except that which is better for thee than what thou dost possess and all the treasures of the earth. Thy Lord, verily, is knowing, informed of all. Arise, in my Name, amongst My servants, and say: 'O ye peoples of the earth! Turn yourselves towards Him Who hath turned towards you. He, verily, is the Face of God amongst you, and His Testimony and His Guide unto you. He hath come to you with signs which none can produce.' The voice of the Burning Bush is raised in the midmost heart of the world, and the Holy Spirit calleth aloud among the nations: 'Lo, the Desired One is come with manifest dominion!'

It is reported that upon receipt of this first message, that arrogant, pride-intoxicated monarch flung down the Tablet saying, 'If this man is God, I am two Gods!' Upon hearing this, Bahá'u'lláh sent another Tablet, through the French agent in 'Akká, severely reprimanding Napoleon, confronting him with his hypocrisy and telling him his punishment.

O King! We heard the words thou didst utter in answer to the Czar of Russia, concerning the decision made regarding the war [Crimean War]. Thy Lord, verily, knoweth, is informed of all. Thou didst say: 'I lay asleep upon my couch, when the cry of the oppressed, who were drowned in the Black Sea, wakened me.' This is what we heard thee say, and, verily, thy Lord is witness unto what I say. We testify that that which wakened thee was not their cry but the promptings of thine own passions, for We tested thee, and found thee wanting . . . Hadst thou been sincere in thy words, thou wouldst have not cast behind thy back the Book of God, when it was sent unto thee by Him Who is the Almighty, the All-Wise. We have proved thee through it, and found thee other than that which thou didst profess . . . For what thou hast done, thy kingdom shall be thrown into confusion, and thine empire shall pass from thine hands, as a punishment for that which thou hast wrought. Then wilt thou know how thou hast plainly erred. Commotions shall seize all the people in that land, unless thou arisest to help this Cause, and followest Him Who is the Spirit of God [Jesus Christ] in this, the Straight Path. Hath thy pomp made thee proud? By My Life! It shall not endure; nay, it shall soon pass away, unless thou holdest fast by this firm Cord. We see abasement hastening after thee, whilst thou art of the heedless. It behoveth thee when thou hearest His Voice calling from the seat of glory to cast away all that thou possessest, and cry out: 'Here am I, O Lord of all that is in heaven and all that is on earth!'[5]

Within months of the receipt of this second Tablet, the battle of Sedan took place and Napoleon III went down to crushing defeat. The empire collapsed, the republic was proclaimed, France was engulfed in disaster and civil war and the proud erstwhile emperor ended his days in ignominious exile.

The dire prophecies made to Kaiser Wilhelm I have been all

too tragically fulfilled in our own day by the two successive world wars, the first of which terminated in the overthrow and extinction of the Hohenzollern dynasty.

O King of Berlin! Give ear unto the Voice calling from this manifest Temple: Verily, there is none other God but Me, the Everlasting, the Peerless, the Ancient of Days. Take heed lest pride debar thee from recognizing the Dayspring of Divine Revelation, lest earthly desires shut thee out, as by a veil, from the Lord of the Throne above and of the earth below. Thus counselleth thee the Pen of the Most High. He, verily, is the Most Gracious, the All-Bountiful. Do thou remember the one whose power transcended thy power [Napoleon III], and whose station excelled thy station. Where is he? Whither are gone the things he possessed? Take warning, and be not of them that are fast asleep. He it was who cast the Tablet of God behind him, when We made known unto him what the hosts of tyranny had caused Us to suffer. Wherefore, disgrace assailed him from all sides, and he went down to dust in great loss. Think deeply, O King, concerning him, and concerning them who, like unto thee, have conquered cities and ruled over men. The All-Merciful brought them down from their palaces to their graves. Be warned, be of them who reflect . . . O banks of the Rhine! We have seen you covered with gore, inasmuch as the swords of retribution were drawn against you; and you shall have another turn. And We hear the lamentations of Berlin, though she be today in conspicuous glory.

A similar humiliation was inflicted upon Pope Pius IX, who held in the religious sphere the same august position as had Napoleon III in the political. Bahá'u'lláh's Tablet to him was sent from Adrianople at a time when the Papal States (the states of the Church) were the sole insignificant remnant of the once vast temporal power of the Papacy. Pius IX was determined to preserve that remaining temporal authority. Bahá'u'lláh wrote to him:

O Pope! Rend the veils asunder. He Who is the Lord of Lords is come overshadowed with clouds, and the decree hath been fulfilled by God, the Almighty, the Unrestrained . . . He verily, hath again come down from Heaven even as He came down from it the first time. Beware that thou dispute not with Him even as the Pharisees disputed with Him [Jesus] without a clear token or proof . . . Arise in the name of thy Lord, the God of Mercy, amidst the peoples of the earth, and seize thou the Cup of Life with the hands of confidence, and first drink thou therefrom, and proffer it then to such as turn towards it amongst the peoples of all faiths . . .

The Word which the Son concealed is made manifest. It hath been sent down in the form of the human temple in this day. Blessed be the Lord Who is the Father! He, verily, is come unto the nations in His most great majesty. Turn your faces towards Him, O concourse of the righteous . . . This is the day whereon the Rock (Peter) crieth out and shouteth, and celebrateth the praise of its Lord, the All-Possessing, the Most High, saying: 'Lo! The Father is come, and that which ye were promised in the Kingdom is fulfilled! . . .'

O Supreme Pontiff! Incline thine ear unto that which the Fashioner of mouldering bones counselleth thee, as voiced by Him Who is His Most Great Name. Sell all the embellished ornaments thou dost possess, and expend them in the path of God, Who causeth the night to return upon the day, and the day to return upon the night. Abandon thy kingdom unto the kings, and emerge from thy habitation, with thy face set towards the Kingdom, and, detached from the world, then speak forth the praises of thy Lord betwixt earth and heaven . . . Beware lest thou appropriate unto thyself the things of the world and the riches thereof. Leave them unto such as desire them, and cleave unto that which hath been enjoined upon thee by Him Who is the Lord of creation. Should any one offer thee all the treasures of the earth, refuse to even glance upon them. Be as thy Lord hath been.

Pius IX disdained to reply. In 1870, after receipt of that Tablet, he issued the famous Bull which proclaimed the new dogma of Papal Infallibility. In that same year, which had witnessed the downfall of Napoleon III, King Victor Emanuel II attacked the Papal States and seized and occupied Rome. Pius IX raised the white flag on the Dome of St Peter and after a thousand years 'the Eternal City' became the seat of a new political entity, the Kingdom of Italy. Pius IX became the 'first prisoner of the Vatican', and its tiny enclave all that remained of the ancient Papal dominions. This shattering blow at the ancient heart of Christendom was but a prelude to even greater catastrophes in the course of the next half century as the influence of its religious establishments was swept away in a wave of secularism and unbelief.

To Náṣiri'd-Dín Sháh, the despotic ruler of Persia, whose reign is forever stained by the orders given for the execution of the Báb, the incarceration of Bahá'u'lláh in the Síyáh-Chál, His subsequent banishment in spite of His recognized innocence and the reign of terror let loose upon the Bábís, Bahá'u'lláh revealed a Tablet, the lengthiest of those addressed to any single ruler. In it He called the Shah's attention to the afflictions which He had suffered in the path of God and requested him to call a meeting of 'the divines of the age' when, in the presence of His Majesty He would produce proofs of His mission and expose the perversity of the ecclesiastic leaders. He urged the Shah to rule with justice and described how God's summons had reached Him in the Síyáh-Chál:

O King! I was but a man like others, asleep upon My couch, when lo, the breezes of the All-Glorious were wafted over Me, and taught Me the knowledge of all that hath been. This thing is not from Me, but from One Who is Almighty and All-Knowing. And He bade Me lift up My voice between earth and heaven, and for this there befell Me what hath caused the tears of every man of understanding to flow. The learning current amongst men I studied not; their schools I entered not. Ask of the city wherein I dwelt, that thou mayest be well assured that I am not of them who speak falsely. This is but a leaf which the winds of the will of thy Lord, the Almighty, the All-Praised, have stirred. Can it be still when the tempestuous winds are blowing? Nay, by Him Who is the Lord of all Names and Attributes! They move it as they list. The evanescent is as nothing before Him Who is the Ever-Abiding. His all-compelling summons hath reached Me, and caused Me to speak His praise amidst all people. I was indeed as one dead when His behest was uttered. The hand of the will of thy Lord, the Compassionate, the Merciful, transformed Me. Can any one speak forth of his own accord that for which all men, both high and low, will protest against him? Nay, by Him Who taught the Pen the eternal mysteries, save him whom the grace of the Almighty, the All-Powerful, hath strengthened. The Pen of the Most High addresseth Me saying: Fear not. Relate unto His Majesty the Sháh that which befell thee.

This Tablet, although revealed in Adrianople, was not delivered until after Bahá'u'lláh's arrival in 'Akká, when He chose a youth of seventeen, whom He named Badí' (Wonderful) to carry it to Teheran and deliver it to the monarch. The story of Badí' is indeed wonderful, tragic and glorious. He made the four-month journey on foot, approached the Shah as he was setting out on a hunting expedition, and called out, 'O King! I have come to thee from Sheba with a weighty message'.[6] He was arrested, tortured for three days with the bastinado and branding irons after which his head was pulverized. Throughout, he steadfastly refused to give the names of any Bahá'ís and laughed in the face of his torturers. Bahá'u'lláh's Tablet had been taken from him and given to the Shah, who sent it to the chief ecclesiastics of Teheran with the command to answer it. They produced no reply but recommended that the bearer be put to death. Some time later the Shah sent the Tablet to his ambassador in Constantinople as an aid to his efforts to excite the hatred of the Sultan's minister against Bahá'u'lláh.

Náṣiri'd-Dín, whom Bahá'u'lláh named 'Prince of oppressors' who had 'perpetrated what hath caused the denizens of the cities of justice and equity to lament'[7] was assassinated on the eve of his jubilee, and the infamous Qajar dynasty, as prophesied by Bahá'u'lláh,* shortly thereafter came to an end.

To the Czar, Alexander II, Bahá'u'lláh acknowledged the help which the Russian ambassador had rendered in freeing Him from the Síyáh-Chál. 'Whilst I lay chained and fettered in the prison, one of thy ministers extended to Me his aid. Wherefore hath God ordained for thee a station which the knowledge of none can comprehend except His knowledge.' He summoned him to proclaim the news of His advent:

---

* 'Before long, you will see the name of the Qájárs obliterated, and the land of Írán cleansed of them.' See Balyuzi, *Bahá'u'lláh, The King of Glory*, p.410.

Arise thou amongst men in the name of this all-compelling Cause, and summon, then, the nations unto God, the Exalted, the Great . . . Say: This is an Announcement whereat the hearts of the Prophets and Messengers have rejoiced. This is the One Whom the heart of the world remembereth and is promised in the Books of God, the Mighty, the All-Wise . . . Say: I, verily, have not sought to extol Mine Own Self, but rather God Himself were ye to judge fairly. Naught can be seen in Me except God and His Cause, could ye but perceive it. I am the One Whom the tongue of Isaiah hath extolled, the One with Whose name both the Torah and the Evangel were adorned . . .

Three times Bahá'u'lláh warned him:

Beware lest thy desire deter thee from turning towards the face of thy Lord, the Compassionate, the Most Merciful. We, verily, have heard the thing for which thou didst supplicate thy Lord, whilst secretly communing with Him . . . Beware lest thou barter away this sublime station . . . Beware lest thy sovereignty withhold thee from Him Who is the Supreme Sovereign.

The Czar made no response to this divine summons and warning but rather pursued his harsh policy of repression against the growing liberalism of the new age. He succumbed to an assassin's bullet and his government continued its way towards the revolution which terminated the dynasty of the Romanoffs, brought chaos and disaster and a fiercer tyranny to the empire of the Czars, resulting seventy years after in the present upheavals and economic breakdown.

The Emperor of Austria, Franz Joseph, heir to the Holy Roman Empire, was reproved by Bahá'u'lláh for ignoring Him while he visited Jerusalem. His reign was the most disastrous in the history of the nation and ended in the disintegration of the empire and the extinction of yet another dynasty, the Hapsburg.

Bahá'u'lláh's Tablet to Queen Victoria is unique in several respects. It is highly commendatory in tone – 'Thou, indeed, hast done well' – and assures the Queen of stability in her affairs. The British legislature and the elected representatives of the people in every land are counselled; the kings of the earth are severely reprimanded and urged to establish the Lesser Peace by means of the principle of collective security of which they are informed. In this Tablet Bahá'u'lláh makes some of His weightiest pronouncements on the whole subject of peace and particularly the Lesser Peace towards which the world is now being so forcefully propelled.

O Queen in London! Incline thine ear unto the voice of thy Lord, the Lord of all mankind, calling from the Divine Lote-Tree: Verily, no God is there but Me, the Almighty, the All-Wise! Cast away all that is on earth, and attire the head of thy kingdom with the crown of the remembrance of thy Lord, the All-Glorious. He, in truth, hath come unto the world in His most great glory, and all that hath been mentioned in the Gospel hath been fulfilled . . .

To the members of the British Parliament:

We have also heard that thou hast entrusted the reins of counsel into the hands of the representatives of the people. Thou, indeed, hast done well, for thereby the foundations of the edifice of thine affairs will be strengthened, and the hearts of all that are beneath thy shadow, whether high or low, will be tranquillized. It behoveth them, however, to be trustworthy among His servants, and to regard themselves as the representatives of all that dwell on earth. This is what counselleth them, in this Tablet, He Who is the Ruler, the All-Wise . . . Blessed is he that entereth the assembly for the sake of God, and judgeth between men with pure justice. He, indeed, is of the blissful . . .

To Parliaments everywhere:

O ye the elected representatives of the people in every land! Take ye counsel together, and let your concern be only for that which profiteth mankind, and bettereth the condition thereof, if ye be of them that scan heedfully. Regard the world as the human body which, though at its creation whole and perfect, hath been afflicted, through various causes, with grave disorders and maladies. Not for one day did it gain ease, nay its sickness waxed more severe, as it fell under the treatment of ignorant physicians, who gave full rein to their personal desires, and have erred grievously. And if, at one time, through the care of an able physician, a member of that body was healed, the rest remained afflicted as before. Thus informeth you the All-Knowing, the All-Wise.

We behold it, in this day, at the mercy of rulers so drunk with pride that they cannot discern clearly their own best advantage, much less recognize a Revelation so bewildering and challenging as this. And whenever any one of them hath striven to improve its condition, his motive hath been his own gain, whether confessedly so or not; and the unworthiness of this motive hath limited his power to heal or cure.

That which the Lord hath ordained as the sovereign remedy and mightiest instrument for the healing of all the world is the union of all its peoples in one universal Cause, one common Faith. This can in no wise be achieved except through the power of a skilled, an all-powerful and inspired Physician.

The Tablet closes with a prayer revealed especially for the Queen:

Turn thou unto God and say: O my Sovereign Lord! I am but a vassal of Thine, and Thou art, in truth, the King of Kings. I have lifted my suppliant hands unto the heaven of Thy grace and Thy bounties. Send down, then, upon me from the clouds of Thy generosity that which will rid me of all save Thee, and draw me nigh unto Thyself. I beseech Thee, O my Lord, by Thy name, which Thou hast made the king of names, and the manifestation of Thyself to all who are in heaven and on earth, to rend asunder the veils that have intervened between me and my recognition of the Dawning-Place of Thy signs and the Day Spring of Thy Revelation. Thou art, verily, the Almighty, the All-Powerful, the All-Bounteous. Deprive me not, O my Lord, of the fragrances of the Robe of Thy mercy in Thy days, and write down for me that which Thou has written down for thy handmaidens who have believed in Thee and in Thy signs, and have recognized Thee, and set their hearts towards the horizon of Thy Cause. Thou art truly the Lord of the worlds and of those who show mercy the Most Merciful. Assist me, then, O my God, to remember Thee amongst Thy handmaidens, and to aid Thy Cause in Thy lands. Accept, then, that which hath escaped me when the light of Thy countenance shone forth. Thou, indeed, hast power over all things. Glory be to Thee, O Thou in Whose hand is the kingdom of the heavens and of the earth.

It is reported that Queen Victoria, upon receiving this Tablet remarked: 'If this is of God it will endure; if not it can do no harm.'[8]

In 1873 when Bahá'u'lláh revealed the *Kitáb-i-Aqdas* from within the walls of the prison-city of 'Akká, the two continents of America were far more occupied with their own affairs than those of the world in general. The possibility of the northern continent becoming the homeland of the richest and most militarily powerful nation on earth was not envisioned, while the central and southern parts were primarily engaged in obtaining their independence from European sovereignty. Throughout the whole vast area, north and south, the native inhabitants were subjugated and despoiled. Yet it was to this decidedly promising but as yet not fully-explored new world that Bahá'u'lláh directed the most sublime responsibilities of human government, the promotion of justice, the remembrance of God, the raising of the fallen and the punishment of the tyrant.

Hearken ye, O Rulers of America and the Presidents of the Republics therein, unto that which the Dove is warbling on the Branch of Eternity: There is none other God but Me, the Ever-Abiding, the Forgiving, the All-Bountiful. Adorn ye the temple of dominion with the ornament of justice and of the fear of God, and its head with the crown of the remembrance of your Lord, the Creator of the heavens . . .

Bind ye the broken with the hands of justice, and crush the oppressor who flourisheth with the rod of the commandments of your Lord, the Ordainer, the All-Wise.

These noble pursuits are consonant with the American dream of the brotherhood of man and certainly with the compassionate words engraved on the Statue of Liberty, gazing across the vast Atlantic towards that old world where the

Manifestations of God have appeared and the great civilizations have risen and declined:

Give me your tired, your poor,
Your huddled masses yearning to breathe free,
The wretched refuse of your teeming shore.

Alas! Alas, that the great American republic has denied religion any function in state affairs and relegated it to the realm of personal matters. Inevitably there has grown an attitude of 'nothing sacred', the golden calf is worshipped and America has led the world into the permissive age. Will she not come to herself, listen to that call from the fortress prison of 'Akká and turn again to those spiritual qualities which laid the foundation of her greatness and which she must again exemplify if she is to lead the nations into the new age?

The overthrow of those kings and emperors who sustained individually the impact of Bahá'u'lláh's declaration and either rejected or ignored His call has been followed by a general decline in the fortunes of kingship, reducing the authority and majesty of the dwindling number of royal thrones. A similar but even more severe deterioration has overtaken, and continues to undermine, the world's chief ecclesiastical thrones and the authority and status of priests. The extinction of the Caliphate, the most powerful institution, religious or secular, in the entire Islamic world, the final reduction of the temporal sovereignty of the papacy to the insignificant area of the Vatican, followed directly in the first case upon its fierce opposition to and persecution of Bahá'u'lláh, and in the case of the Pontiff upon his rejection of the summons and clear warnings addressed to him by the Lord of lords. The leaders of both Christianity and Islam, the 'false prophets' who have failed to recognize the promised Qá'im, the return of Christ, or even to examine His Cause as He called upon them to do, have suffered a decline in the hundred years since His proclamation to them, unparallelled in religious history. The once-powerful princes of the church, the bishops with their hierachies of priests, greatly reduced in number and even more in status and influence, refusing the new message from God which the Gospel taught them to expect, have relapsed further and further into relics of a former age, their palaces and episcopates equivalent to the great castles which once asserted the ascendancy of the barons. The wonderful cathedrals of Europe, built to the glory of Christ, have become tourist attractions, history museums and the home of musical and other artistic presentations, and in some a charge is made for entry.

Bahá'u'lláh addressed the priests and people of all religions, but specifically those of Judaism, Christendom, Islam and Zoroastrianism.

At one time We address the people of the Torah and summon them unto Him Who is the Revealer of verses, Who hath come from Him Who layeth low the necks of men . . . At another, We address the people of the Evangel and say: 'The All-Glorious is come in this Name whereby the Breeze of God hath wafted over all regions' . . . At still another, We address the people of the Qur'án saying: 'Fear the All-Merciful, and cavil not at Him through Whom all religions were founded' . . . Know thou, moreover, that We have addressed to the Magians Our Tablets, and adorned them with Our Law . . . We have revealed in them the essence of all the hints and allusions contained in their Books. The Lord, verily, is the Almighty, the All-Knowing.

To the Jews He wrote:

The Most Great Law is come, and the Ancient Beauty ruleth upon the throne of David. . . . Lend an ear unto the song of David. He saith: 'Who will bring me into the Strong City?' The Strong City is 'Akká, which hath been named the Most Great Prison, and which possesseth a fortress and mighty ramparts . . . Peruse that which Isaiah hath spoken in His Book. He saith: 'Get thee up into the high mountain, O Zion, that bringest good tidings; lift up thy voice with strength, O Jerusalem, that bringest good tidings. Lift it up, be not afraid; say unto the cities of Judah: "Behold your God! Behold the Lord God will come with strong hand, and His arm shall rule for

Him." ' This Day all the signs have appeared. A great City hath descended from heaven, and Zion trembleth and exulteth with joy at the Revelation of God, for it hath heard the Voice of God on every side.

To the high priests of Zoroastrianism He declared:

O high priests! Ears have been given you that they may hearken unto the mystery of Him Who is the Self-Dependent, and eyes that they may behold Him. Wherefore flee ye? The Incomparable Friend is manifest. He speaketh that wherein lieth salvation. Were ye, O high priests, to discover the perfume of the rose-garden of understanding, ye would seek none other but Him, and would recognize, in His new vesture, the All-Wise and Peerless One, and would turn your eyes from the world and all who seek it, and would arise to help Him.

In innumerable passages throughout the great volume of His revelation He addresses the various categories of priests and leaders of different religious communities. To those of Christendom He writes:

O Concourse of archbishops! He Who is the Lord of all men hath appeared. In the plain of guidance He calleth mankind, whilst ye are numbered with the dead! Great is the blessedness of him who is stirred by the Breeze of God, and hath arisen from amongst the dead in this perspicuous Name.

O Concourse of bishops! Ye are the stars of the heaven of My knowledge. My mercy desireth not that ye should fall upon the earth. My justice, however, declareth: 'This is that which the Son [Jesus] hath decreed.' And whatsoever hath proceeded out of His blameless, His truth-speaking, trustworthy mouth, can never be altered. The bells, verily, peal out My Name, and lament over Me, but My spirit rejoiceth with evident gladness. The body of the Loved One yearneth for the cross, and His head is eager for the spear, in the path of the All-Merciful. The ascendancy of the oppressor can in no wise deter Him from His purpose . . . The stars of the heaven of knowledge have fallen, they that adduce the proofs they possess in order to demonstrate the truth of My Cause, and who make mention of God in My name. When I came unto them, in My majesty, however, they turned aside from Me. They, verily, are of the fallen. This is what the Spirit [Jesus] prophesied when He came with the truth, and the Jewish doctors cavilled at Him, until they committed what made the Holy Spirit to lament, and the eyes of such as enjoy near access to God to weep.

The 'Concourse of patriarchs' are addressed, the 'Concourse of monks', the 'Concourse of priests', the 'divines', all Christians:

O concourse of Christians! . . . We, verily, have come for your sakes, and have borne the misfortunes of the world for your salvation. Flee ye the One Who hath sacrificed His life that ye may be quickened? Fear God, O followers of the Spirit [Jesus], and walk not in the footsteps of every divine that hath gone far astray . . . Open the doors of your hearts. He Who is the Spirit [Jesus] verily, standeth before them. Wherefore keep ye afar from Him Who hath purposed to draw you nigh unto a Resplendent Spot? Say: We, in truth, have opened unto you the gates of the Kingdom. Will ye bar the doors of your houses in My face? This indeed is naught but a grievous error.

O kings of Christendom! Heard ye not the saying of Jesus, the Spirit of God, 'I go away, and come again unto you'? Wherefore, then, did ye fail, when He did come again unto you in the clouds of heaven, to draw nigh unto Him, that ye might behold His face, and be of them that attained His Presence? In another passage He saith: 'When He, the Spirit of Truth, is come, He will guide you into all truth.' And yet, behold how, when He did bring the truth, ye refused to turn your faces towards Him, and persisted in disporting yourselves with your pastimes and fancies. Ye welcomed Him not, neither did ye seek His Presence, that ye might hear the verses of God from His own mouth, and partake of the manifold wisdom of the Almighty, the All-Glorious, the All-Wise. Ye have, by reason of your failure, hindered the breath of God from being wafted over you, and have withheld from your souls the sweetness of its fragrance. Ye continue roving with delight in the valley of your corrupt desires. Ye, and all ye possess shall pass away. Ye shall, most certainly, return to God, and shall be called to account for your doings in the presence of Him Who shall gather together the entire creation . . . [9]

Followers of the Gospel, behold the gates of heaven are flung open. He that had ascended unto it is now come. Give ear to His voice calling aloud over land and sea, announcing to all mankind the advent of this Revelation – a Revelation through the agency of which the Tongue of Grandeur is now proclaiming: 'Lo, the sacred Pledge hath been fulfilled, for He, the Promised One is come!'[10]

To the divines of Sunni Islam He declared:

Because of you the Apostle [Muḥammad] lamented, and the Chaste One [Fáṭimih] cried out, and the countries were laid waste, and darkness fell upon all regions. O concourse of divines! Because of you the people were abased, and the banner of Islám was hauled down, and its mighty throne subverted. Every time a man of discernment hath sought to hold fast unto that which would exalt Islám, you raised a clamour, and thereby was He deterred from achieving his purpose, while the land remained fallen in clear ruin.

To the Shi'ahs:

O concourse of Persian divines! In My name ye have seized the reins of men, and occupy the seats of honour by reason of your relation to Me. When I revealed Myself, however, ye turned aside, and committed what hath caused the tears of such as have recognized Me to flow. Erelong will all that ye possess perish, and your glory be turned into the most wretched abasement, and ye shall behold the punishment for what ye have wrought, as decreed by God, the Ordainer, the All-Wise.

Bahá'u'lláh dwelt at length upon the spiritual blindness, bigotry and arrogance of the ecclesiastical establishments at the time of the appearance of God's Messengers.

Leaders of religion, in every age, have hindered their people from attaining the shores of eternal salvation, inasmuch as they held the reins of authority in their mighty grasp. Some for the lust of leadership, others through want of knowledge and understanding, have been the cause of the deprivation of the people. By their sanction and authority, every Prophet of God hath drunk from the chalice of sacrifice, and winged His flight unto the heights of glory. What unspeakable cruelties they that have occupied the seats of authority and learning have inflicted upon the true Monarchs of the world, those Gems of divine virtue!'[11]

We recall that Abraham was cast into fire by the 'divines of the age'; Moses was opposed by Pharaoh's priests who spread lies and calumnies about Him; Annas and Caiaphas, the chief priests of Judaism, with the Pharisees, brought about the crucifixion of Jesus; the idolatrous priests of Arabia persecuted Muhammad when He proclaimed the unity of God; the whole authority of Shi'ah Islam combined to execute the Báb; and Bahá'u'lláh bore such sufferings and cruelty as none can assess.

Little wonder that He should decree:

O concourse of divines! Ye shall not henceforth behold yourselves possessed of any power, inasmuch as We have seized it from you, and destined it for such as have believed in God, the One, the All-Powerful, the Almighty, the Unconstrained.

Nevertheless,

Great is the blessedness of that divine that hath not allowed knowledge to become a veil between him and the One Who is the Object of all knowledge, and who, when the Self-Subsisting appeared, hath turned with a beaming face towards Him.

Likewise,

The pious deeds of the monks and priests among the followers of the Spirit [Jesus] . . . are remembered in His presence.[12]

Such was Bahá'u'lláh's proclamation to those who controlled the destinies of the greater part of the human race, yet this was but a wave from the mighty ocean of His announcement. The appalling responsibility which rests on the shoulders of those arrogant obscurantists who either, like Náṣiri'd-Dín Sháh, tortured and killed His messenger, or rejected, scorned or ignored His message, may be measured by the 'divine chastisement' which so swiftly reduced their pride and obliterated their dominion. Bahá'u'lláh commented to Queen Victoria that He saw the world

at the mercy of rulers so drunk with pride that they cannot discern clearly their own best advantage, much less recognize a Revelation so bewildering and challenging as this.

He warned them in ominous tones of the disastrous consequences which their rejection of Him and His message would entail and finally pronounced His judgement against them:

From two ranks amongst men power hath been seized: kings and ecclesiastics. [13]

He ordains that priesthood will not be re-established, but He does not wish mankind to be deprived of kingship, which He declares to be a sign of the majesty of God. He eulogizes that monarch who will rule with justice and compassion and He foresees the appearance of constitutional sovereigns who will be emblems of wisdom and justice.

Chapter 15

ADRIANOPLE AND THE LAST BANISHMENT

THE overwhelming vanity and ambition of Mírzá Yaḥyá, together with his moral turpitude, made him the ready tool for the accomplishment of Siyyid Muḥammad's machinations against Bahá'u'lláh. Mírzá Yaḥyá was not only the nominated head of the Bábí community, he was also Bahá'u'lláh's half-brother. The Bábís were more than willing to accord him the respect, and even love, which such a high station would naturally command. But Yaḥyá's cowardice was the prime cause of his undoing. After the martyrdom of the Báb he did nothing to rally, or help in any way the distressed Bábís, but went into hiding and forbade the Bábís to seek him out or even recognize him should they see him.

This Siyyid Muḥammad-i-Iṣfáhání was an archetype of that strange human perversity which hates the light and all that is good. It is compounded of envy and pride and manifests itself in a passionate hatred for all who strive to raise humanity to that station of spiritual nobility for which it was created. Siyyid Muḥammad set himself to destroy Bahá'u'lláh, using Mírzá Yaḥyá as his despised but willing tool, and has found his place in history as the antichrist of the Bahá'í Dispensation.

We may pause to reflect that this eternal battle between God and the human egotistic will, characterized in simpler times as Satan, is fought in every dispensation. God's Manifestation is always victorious and Satan succumbs, enabling the lights of justice, honour and decency to irradiate a new civilization. But after a time, as the love of God grows cold, Satan raises his head. The once civilized society declines and enters a permissive age and all the false gods of Mammon preside over an 'abomination of desolation'. It is then that the Manifestation of God reappears to heal the sick body of the world, to bear the burden of its concentrated evil (the sins of the world) and to defeat once more the Prince of Darkness. These ancient, much ridiculed clichés exhibit new life as the Sun of Truth restores mankind to spiritual consciousness, while the apocalyptic struggle which they attempt to envision is symbolized again in the circumstantial events attending the earthly life of the Manifestation of God.

A recital of the intrigues, crimes and plots undertaken by Yaḥyá at the instigation of Siyyid Muḥammad would be wearisome and unedifying. It includes murder, libel, subversion, misrepresentation to authority, appeals to Bahá'u'lláh's known enemies, attempts at assassination and corruption of the text of the Báb's revelation. A blatant and naive attempt at portraying himself as the Báb's successor, by interpolating into His writings references to a succession which nominated Yaḥyá and his descendants as heirs of the Báb, was compounded by the blasphemous addition of a passage in the call to prayer which identified himself with the Godhead. In Adrianople he poisoned the well which supplied water to Bahá'u'lláh and His family, and actually poisoned the cup of tea to which he had invited Bahá'u'lláh. It caused a serious illness, lasting a month, and left Bahá'u'lláh with a shaking hand for the rest of His life. He circulated rumours among the Bábís in Persia discreditable to Bahá'u'lláh which caused confusion and distress among them just as they were beginning to hear the news of His Declaration in the Garden of Riḍván. Bahá'u'lláh concealed as far as possible these criminal activities and played down the enmity of His half-brother, but when Yaḥyá attempted to bribe the barber, Ustád Muḥammad, to assassinate Bahá'u'lláh while attending Him in the bath, that staunch soul was so enraged that in spite of the admonitions of both Bahá'u'lláh and 'Abdu'l-Bahá he was unable to keep himself from telling what had happened. The community of exiles was plunged into consternation.

Bahá'u'lláh now took action. He sent His amanuensis to Mírzá Yahyá, bearing a copy of His recently revealed *Súriy-i-Amr* (Tablet of Command), which stated in clear language His claims and their implications of recognition and submission to the Will of God. The amanuensis was instructed to read it aloud to Yahyá and demand 'an unequivocal and conclusive reply'.[1] Yahyá's request for a day's respite, enabling him to meditate his reply, was granted.

The reply, when it came, was a counter-declaration asserting that he, Mírzá Yahyá, had received an independent revelation from God, which required the unqualified submission to him of the entire population of the earth.

This blasphemous statement precipitated the complete rupture between Bahá'u'lláh and Yahyá, although a pilgrim Bábí from Shiraz attempted to arrange a public confrontation, and extracted a promise from Yahyá to appear at the mosque of Sultán Salím. Bahá'u'lláh went on foot to the appointment but Yahyá did not come. To the great relief of the exiles, Mírzá Yahyá was expelled from the community; and he and his family, with Siyyid Muhammad and one other who had associated himself with them, became known as Azalís, from a title, Subh-i-Azal (Morning of Eternity), used by him.

This entire episode was the cause of great anguish to Bahá'u'lláh. He lamented:

He who for months and years I reared with the hand of loving-kindness hath risen to take My life . . . The cruelties inflicted by My oppressors have bowed Me down, and turned My hair white. Shouldst thou present thyself before My throne, thou wouldst fail to recognize the Ancient Beauty, for the freshness of His countenance is altered, and its brightness hath faded, by reason of the oppression of the infidels.[2]

This is the moment to recall that the Divine Messenger, the Manifestation of God, never uses His supreme and irresistible power to shield His human personality or physical body from the cruelties, scorn, humiliations, even death which the world invariably heaps upon Him. At the same time His compassion is boundless and extended to the most inveterate and bitter of His enemies. Six years after Mírzá Yahyá's demission Bahá'u'lláh addressed him in the *Kitáb-i-Aqdas*, the Most Holy Book

. . . fear not because of thy deeds . . . return unto God, humble, submissive and lowly . . . He will put away from thee thy sins . . . thy Lord is the Forgiving, the Mighty, the All-Merciful.[3]

The damage which Yahyá's conduct had done to the infant Faith and its growing Order would continue to stain its name for a further half-century and beyond the confines of Turkey. The lies and calumnies which he had circulated in Constantinople, in no way lessened by the perfidious Persian ambassador, to whom Siyyid Muhammad had made a personal visit in order to vilify Bahá'u'lláh, perplexed and cast doubts into the minds of those highly-placed people who had been so impressed by Bahá'u'lláh's dignified conduct in the capital. The prestige of the Faith was lessened in the eyes of its western admirers, such as E. G. Browne and A. L. M. Nicolas, the French diplomat and translator of the Persian and Arabic Bayáns.

Yahyá's campaign among the Bábís of Persia and Iraq, calumniating Bahá'u'lláh and elevating himself beyond anything which the Báb's nomination specified, caused confusion within their ranks. They knew nothing of Yahyá except that he was nominated by the Báb as head of the Bábí community. Why then did he not rejoice with them at the appearance of 'He Whom God shall make manifest'? Many were sorely perplexed and great discussions were held among them. A few became partisans of Yahyá and separated themselves from the Bahá'ís. But by 1912, twenty years after Bahá'u'lláh's ascension, when Yaḥyá died in lonely ignominy, with none to bury him either as a Bábí or a Bahá'í, the Azalís were not in evidence, while the steadfast and rapidly growing Bahá'í community, under the protection of Bahá'u'lláh's Covenant and the incomparable guidance of His eldest Son, the Centre of that Covenant and appointed successor of His almighty Father, was beginning to encircle the globe.

Bahá'u'lláh revealed the *Tablet of Aḥmad*, and sent it to its recipient Aḥmad-i-Yazdí, a resident of Baghdad who was in Constantinople on his way to Adrianople to see again his beloved Lord. He was one of those extraordinarily blessed souls who had attained the presence of the Báb and Bahá'u'lláh, and had actually lived for six years in an outer portion of Bahá'u'lláh's house in Baghdad. Upon reading his Tablet 'he knew what was expected of him' and immediately returned to Persia and devoted himself to conveying Bahá'u'lláh's message to the Bábí community there.

In this Tablet Bahá'u'lláh removed the perplexities of the Bábís and confirmed their faith in Himself. He assures them that the Báb 'was the true One from God, to Whose commands we are all conforming'.

Of Himself He declares:

Verily this is that Most Great Beauty, foretold in the Books of the Messengers, through Whom truth shall be distinguished from error and the wisdom of every command shall be tested. Verily He is the Tree of Life that bringeth forth the fruits of God, the Exalted, the Powerful, the Great.

Aḥmad travelled throughout Persia, reciting this Tablet to the Bábís, confirming that Bahá'u'lláh was indeed 'He Whom God shall make manifest', and the Promised One of all ages. Aḥmad was also able to refer them to a written statement of the Báb's which declared that 'He Whom God shall make manifest' would bear the name Bahá.*

---

* See Taherzadeh. *The Revelation of Bahá'u'lláh*, vol. 2, chap. 5. Oxford: George Ronald, 1977.

This *Tablet of Aḥmad** is one of the best-known, most widely spread, best loved and most frequently recited of all Bahá'u'lláh's prayers and homilies. It opens, as do many of His writings, with mention of God:

He is the King, the All-Knowing, the Wise!

There follows immediately a metaphor, unmistakable in its meaning to all Persians and utterly charming to one even slightly acquainted with the rich symbolism of Persian literature:

Lo, the Nightingale of Paradise singeth upon the twigs of the Tree of Eternity, with holy and sweet melodies . . .

It was through the influence of this Tablet that Bahá'u'lláh imbued the Bahá'ís of Persia, as distinct from their fellow countrymen at that time, with the same heroism and fortitude under appalling torture that the Bábís before them had displayed and which had moved Lord Curzon to testify in his *Persia and the Persian Question*, 'Tales of magnificent heroism illumine the blood-stained pages of Bábí history . . . The fires of Smithfield† did not kindle a nobler courage than has met and defied the more refined torture-mongers of Ṭihrán.'[4] Bahá'u'lláh's admonition was:

. . . be thou so steadfast in My love that thy heart shall not waver, even if the swords of the enemies rain blows upon thee and all the heavens and the earth arise against thee.

Later in the Tablet He wrote, confirming the essential oneness of all the Manifestations of God:

Be thou assured in thyself that verily, he who turns away from this Beauty hath also turned away from the Messengers of the past and showeth pride towards God from all eternity to all eternity.

---

* This *Tablet of Aḥmad* is revealed in Arabic. There is another in Persian addressed to one of the exiles whose conduct was unbecoming.
† Smithfield was the area in London where, in earlier times, Catholics and Protestants used to burn each other.

The Tablet concludes with a promise, unique in the written scriptures of the world:

By God! Should one who is in affliction or grief read this Tablet with absolute sincerity, God will dispel his sadness, solve his difficulties and remove his afflictions.

Verily, He is the Merciful, the Compassionate. Praised be to God, the Lord of all the worlds.

This powerful Tablet, a bulwark to faith and courage, a source of strength and hope in the battle of life, is but one of the munificent gifts with which Bahá'u'lláh has endowed His followers.

Many illuminating details about the life of the little band of Bahá'ís in Adrianople are given by H. M. Balyuzi. He presents a picture of a blissful company, spiritualized by their close association with their Lord, unified in their devotion to Him. They were exiles, in straitened circumstances, poorly clothed and poorly housed, faced by a dark, uncertain future, but 'they had attained their heart's desire and were happy'.[5] In their midst moved the majestic, awe-inspiring Figure of the Beloved, gracious, compassionate, loving, the Sun of their existence whose radiance encompassed them all. Bahá'u'lláh's exaltation and ascendancy among men was, as ever, apparent from the moment of His arrival in the city. Even before, during the journey from Constantinople, the captain in charge of the caravan had become His devoted and respectful admirer. A story is told of this man.

His name was 'Alí Big. When he came to take leave of Bahá'u'lláh he mentioned that his great desire was to obtain the rank of major and be posted to Adrianople. Bahá'u'lláh assured him that he would attain his wish, and shortly after he appeared again in Adrianople – Major 'Alí Big, informing everyone that his promotion was a bounty from Bahá'u'lláh. A little later he found himself longing for a higher rank, and once again he approached Bahá'u'lláh. He was assured that the promotion would be his and he is next seen as Colonel 'Alí

Big. Overjoyed, and openly declaring that he owed his good fortune to Bahá'u'lláh, he associated with His followers on all possible occasions. However, it seemed to him that since he had come so far, it would be quite reasonable to go one step further and become a Páshá. But alas, he died before achieving this distinction – Colonel 'Alí Big.

Soon after their arrival Bahá'u'lláh advised the friends to engage in trade. Áqá Ridá had no other desire than to serve Bahá'u'lláh and he thought an occupation might prevent his doing so. However, when all the friends were gathered together one day, Bahá'u'lláh said that He had commanded them to follow trades so that they might be usefully occupied, not get bored, earn some money and invite Him to their celebrations.

We know by name many of this happy band of exiles and as the story unfolds they become our old friends. There was the immortal and ever-faithful Nabíl, chronicler of the Faith from the days of the Báb; Áqá Ridá the confectioner, who wrote his account at the request of Nabíl; Áshchí the cook, who had been taken as an orphan boy to Bahá'u'lláh's home in Baghdad where he grew up and learned his craft and who, on his deathbed in 1924, dictated his story of seventy years; Ustád Muhammad the barber, whom we have already met; Mishkín-Qalam, the world-famous calligrapher; Mírzá Mahmúd-i-Káshání of whom the following story is told. During that first winter of their arrival the exiles suffered greatly from the biting cold and there was a constant changing of accommodation from inadequate house to inadequate house. After some months Bahá'u'lláh said to Mírzá Mahmúd, 'You are a tall man and nearer to God. Pray that He may give us a better house.' A few days later an excellent house became available and Bahá'u'lláh went to view it. He approved it and commented, 'God answered the prayers of Áqá Mírzá Mahmúd'.[6]

This splendid house, named the house of Amru'lláh,* of

* Shoghi Effendi translated this as House of God's command.

three storeys with 'a Turkish bath of its own, with running water in the kitchen' had thirty rooms. Bahá'u'lláh and His family occupied the top floor; Mírzá Muhammad-Qulí, Bahá'u'lláh's half-brother, took the middle one, and some of the attendants the ground floor; an outer quarter (*bírúní*) provided ample accommodation for the rest of the friends and rooms for gatherings and reception. A good house was found nearby for Mírzá Músá and another for Mírzá Yahyá and his family.

'We were all very happy in that house of Amru'lláh,' Áqá Ridá stated.[7] The friends would gather every night and Bahá'u'lláh often visited them.

The Governor of Adrianople, Khurshíd Páshá, and his deputy, 'Azíz Páshá, became very devoted to Bahá'u'lláh, and 'Azíz Páshá called on Him to pay his respects. He became deeply attached to 'Abdu'l-Bahá, then in His early twenties, and later when he had become Válí of Beirut he visited 'Akká twice to show his reverence for Bahá'u'lláh and to refresh his friendship with the Master.

Khurshíd Páshá was eager to entertain Bahá'u'lláh at Government House, but Bahá'u'lláh did not call. One day of Ramadan, however, the Governor had invited the divines and notables of the city to break their fast at his house, and he implored 'Abdu'l-Bahá 'to beg Bahá'u'lláh to honour that great feast and glittering assemblage with His presence. Bahá'u'lláh accepted that invitation. Áshchí relates how the guests, amongst whom were both men of substance and men of high learning, sat spellbound, captivated and exhilarated by Bahá'u'lláh's utterance. Humbly and courteously they asked Him questions which He answered with overwhelming power and authority, to their marvel and complete satisfaction.'[8]

Khurshíd Páshá invited 'Abdu'l-Bahá to spend as many evenings as He could during Ramadan at Government House, an invitation which 'Abdu'l-Bahá accepted.

In addition to the two chief events of the Adrianople period, already described, others of significance to the progress of the

Faith occurred. Shoghi Effendi refers to the emergence of some of those *treasures* promised by God to Bahá'u'lláh as He lay in chains in the Síyáh-Chál. Dedicated and capable believers arose to defend the new-born Faith and to refute the lies and slanders of its fanatical enemies. The banner of the Faith was implanted in the Caucasus and Syria and the first centre was established in Egypt. The Bahá'í community began to take shape with the inception by Bahá'u'lláh of the Pilgrimage and the revelation of prayers related to the annual Fast, both of which observances He would later confirm in the Most Holy Book, the *Kitáb-i-Aqdas*. He gave instructions at this time to two trusted believers in Teheran to remove 'with the utmost secrecy' the remains of the Báb from their place of concealment to another location,[9] whence they would, by long and devious stages, eventually, after sixty years, reach their eternal resting place in the heart of Carmel, at the exact spot which Bahá'u'lláh Himself would designate to 'Abdu'l-Bahá, thus laying the foundation of the spiritual centre of God's Holy Faith on God's Holy Mountain in the Holy Land. In Adrianople the *Tablet of the Branch* was revealed, foreshadowing the unique station of 'Abdu'l-Bahá which would later be defined in the *Book of the Covenant* and confirmed in the *Kitáb-i-Aqdas*, a station which was to hold untold significance for the future of the Faith, its protection from schism, its expansion, the interpretation of its sacred text and its firm establishment in the West.

A few believers had made their way from Persia and Baghdad to join Bahá'u'lláh in Adrianople, among them Nabíl and Mishkín-Qalam, but as time went on, more and more believers undertook journeys of pilgrimage, to see Bahá'u'lláh, enter His presence and return home blessed and confirmed in their faith.

Bahá'u'lláh's relentless enemies, the Persian officials and 'ulamá, Sultán 'Abdu'l-'Azíz and his ministers, were highly gratified by the supreme crisis in the affairs of the Faith brought about by Mírzá Yahyá's open opposition to Bahá'u'lláh and his subsequent expulsion from the ranks of the believers.

Ever watchful for opportunities to inflict further hardship on Bahá'u'lláh and His followers, they now made the increasing flow of pilgrims to Adrianople a cause for alarm. They gave credence to the most incredible and fatuous accusations made by Yahyá, as for instance that Bahá'u'lláh was conspiring with Bulgarian and certain European powers to arm thousands of His followers and capture Constantinople. The Persian government prohibited Bahá'ís from making the pilgrimage and persecutions broke out in many parts of the country; believers in Iraq were attacked, and in Egypt 'a greedy and vicious consul-general' arrested seven Bahá'ís and had them condemned to a nine-year exile in Khartoum. Bahá'u'lláh sent Nabíl to Egypt to plead with the Khedive, but that same consul-general had him arrested and cast into prison. The Persian ambassador in Constantinople, Bahá'u'lláh's old enemy, represented to Fu'ád Páshá that the presence of Bahá'u'lláh in Adrianople, the comparative freedom which His exile allowed and the esteem which successive governors had accorded Him, constituted a grave danger to the state.

'Abdu'l-'Azíz issued the fateful decree. Bahá'u'lláh and His followers were banished to the penal colony of 'Akká and Mírzá Yahyá to Cyprus. 'The Persian Ambassador promptly informed the Persian consuls in 'Iráq and Egypt that the Turkish government had withdrawn its protection from the Bábís, and that they were free to treat them as they pleased'.[10]

One morning, suddenly, without warning, Bahá'u'lláh's house was surrounded by soldiers and all Bahá'ís were ordered to make ready for departure. Great was their consternation. Would they be separated from Bahá'u'lláh? This was their sole concern; the hardships of another exile, the auctioning of their possessions at half their value were as nothing compared with the appalling prospect of separation from Him to Whom they gave a 'devotion and love which kings might envy and emperors sigh for in vain'.[11] Hájí Ja'far-i-Tabrízí, whose name was omitted from the list of exiles who were to accompany Bahá'u'lláh, cut his own throat. He was rescued from death by fellow believers. Bahá'u'lláh visited him, and sitting at his bedside, consoled him, 'Look up to God and be content with His will.'[12] Ja'far recovered and was later sent to 'Akká, to regain the presence of Bahá'u'lláh.

The governor had been vigorously defending Bahá'u'lláh against the charges sent from Constantinople and was so embarrassed by the order for exile that he refused to deliver it and absented himself from his post, leaving instructions for the registrar to inform Bahá'u'lláh of its contents. The notables of the city were greatly distressed and expressed their sorrow; the consuls of European powers called on Bahá'u'lláh in a body and repeatedly offered to intervene with their governments on His behalf. He graciously acknowledged their concern but firmly declined their support, affirming, 'My relief lies in the hands of God. My focus is God, and to Him alone do I turn.'[13] Large numbers of the populace, who had come to admire and respect the exiles, flocked round them expressing sorrow and consolation. Ja'far's attempted suicide aroused their astonishment and curiosity; Áqá Ridá relates their comment, 'What is this attraction which makes them prefer the hardships of banishment, imprisonment and even death rather than separation?' When Bahá'u'lláh came out of His house to take His seat in the wagon they came forward to kiss His hands and the hem of His garments. He Himself testified in the *Súriy-i-Ra'ís*:

The people surrounded the house, and Muslims and Christians wept over Us . . . We perceived that the weeping of the people of the Son [Christians] exceeded the weeping of others – a sign for such as ponder . . . The consuls of that city gathered in the presence of this Youth . . . and expressed their desire to aid Him. They, verily, evinced towards us manifest affection . . . this Youth hath departed out of this country and deposited beneath every tree and every stone a trust, which God will erelong bring forth through the power of truth.[14]

They were taken to Gallipoli where they waited three days

and nights to board the steamer which would take them to Alexandria. There they would tranship to Haifa and thence by sailing vessel across the bay to 'Akká.

At Gallipoli, as they were about to depart, Bahá'u'lláh warned the whole company that greater trials than they had as yet faced were in store for them and it would be better for anyone who did not feel

man enough to face the future [to] depart to whatever place he pleaseth, and be preserved from tests, for hereafter he will find himself unable to leave . . .

'a warning', Shoghi Effendi commented, 'which His companions unanimously chose to disregard.'[15]

There had been much speculation and anxiety among the friends about their eventual disposition. There was talk of all being sent back to Persia, while some thought that the Blessed Perfection, as Bahá'u'lláh had come to be known by the Bahá'ís, and His brothers would be sent to one place and the rest of the company scattered as exiles to various localities. There was even talk of extermination. But their great fear was separation from their Beloved, and when the government's original plan was announced — to send Bahá'u'lláh and His family to 'Akká and the rest to Constantinople — there were 'scenes of indescribable distress'. Bahá'u'lláh intervened, and through the instrumentality of the officer sent to accompany them, 'Umar Effendi, had this plan cancelled. Finally it was decided that Bahá'u'lláh and all His companions — together they numbered some seventy — were to go to the great prison of 'Akká, while Mírzá Yaḥyá and his associates would be sent to Cyprus. It was further stipulated that four of Bahá'u'lláh's companions should accompany Mírzá Yaḥyá and a similar number of Azalís should go with the main body to 'Akká. Among these latter were the infamous Siyyid Muḥammad and Áqá Ján Big*, both of whose propensities for mischief would

---

* Not to be confused with Mírzá Áqá Ján, Bahá'u'lláh's amanuensis.

find fertile outlets in 'Akká and cause further suffering to Bahá'u'lláh.

The voyage to 'Akká was attended by two incidents of pertinence to our story. One is romantic in the classical sense, and, in Nabíl's own account, a delightful example of that mixture of epigram and metaphor which so enriches Persian literature and intrigues the western mind. It also provides a highly illuminated glimpse of the effect produced upon a young Christian by his unexpected encounter with Bahá'u'lláh.

Nabíl was in the prison of Alexandria which overlooked the harbour. Prior to this he had had a dream in which Bahá'u'lláh told him that within eighty-one days he would receive some cause of rejoicing. He made friends with a physician in the prison who 'tried to convert me to the Protestant Faith. We had long talks and he became a Bahá'í.'

On the eighty-first day of my dream, from the roof-top of the prison-house, I caught sight of Áqá Muhammad-Ibráhím-i-Názir, passing through the street. I called out to him and he came up. I asked him what he was doing there, and he told me that the Blessed Perfection and the companions were being taken to 'Akká . . . and that he had come ashore in the company of a policeman to make some purchases. The policeman, he said, 'will not allow me to stop here much longer. I will go and report your presence here to Áqá ['Abdu'l-Bahá]. Should the ship stay here longer, I shall perhaps come and see you again.' He set my being on fire and went away. The physician was not there at the time. When he came, he found me shedding tears, and reciting these lines: 'The Beloved is by my side and I am far away from Him; I am on the shore of the waters of proximity and yet deprived I am. O Friend! Lift me, lift me to a seat on the ship of nearness; I am helpless, I am vanquished, a prisoner am I.' It was in the evening that Fáris (that was the name of the physician) came, and saw my distress. He said, 'You were telling me that on the eighty-first day of your dream you must receive some cause of rejoicing and today is that eighty-first day. Now, on the contrary, I find you greatly disturbed.' I replied, 'Truly that cause for rejoicing has come, but alas! "The date is on the palm-tree and our hands cannot reach it." ' He said, 'Tell me what has happened, perhaps I could do something about it.' And so I told him that the Blessed Perfection was on that boat. He too, like me, was greatly disturbed, and said, 'Were the next day not Friday, and the *Seraye* closed, we could, both of us, have got permission to board the ship and attain His presence. But still, something can be done. You write whatever you wish. I will get these letters to him to take to the liner.' I wrote my story and gathered together all the poems I had composed in the prison. Fáris, the physician, also wrote a letter and stated his great sorrow. It was very touching. All of these he put in an envelope, which he gave to a young watch-maker named Constantine, to deliver early in the morning. I gave him the name of Khádim and some others of the companions, told him how to identify them, and impressed on him not to deliver the envelope until he had found one of them. He went out in the morning. We were looking from the roof-top. We first heard the signal, and then the noise of the movement of the ship, and were perplexed, lest he had not made it. Then the ship stopped, and started again after a quarter of an hour. We were on tenterhooks, when suddenly Constantine arrived. He handed me an envelope and a package in a handkerchief, and exclaimed, 'By God! I saw the Father of Christ.' Fáris, the physician, kissed his eyes and said, 'Our lot was the fire of separation, yours was the bounty of gazing upon the Beloved of the World.' In answer to our petitions, there was a Tablet, in the script of Revelation,* a Letter from the Most Great Branch ['Abdu'l-Bahá] and a paper filled by almond *nuql* [a sweet] sent by the Purest Branch.† In the Tablet, Fáris, the physician, had been particularly honoured. One of the attendants had written: 'Several times I have witnessed evidences of power which I can never forget. And so it was today. The ship was on the move, when we saw a boat far away. The captain stopped the ship, and this young watch-maker reached us, and called aloud my name. We went to him and he gave us your envelope. All eyes were on us and we are exiles. Yet no one questioned the action of the captain.'16

The second incident occurred as Bahá'u'lláh stepped into the boat which would carry Him to the sea gate of 'Akká, through

---

* The private shorthand of the amanuensis.
† 'Abdu'l-Bahá's younger brother, Mírzá Mihdí, who would die in the prison of 'Akká, aged 22.

which He would enter the city. 'Abdu'l-Ghaffár, one of those four companions named to accompany Yaḥyá to Cyprus, whom Bahá'u'lláh had praised for his 'detachment, love and trust in God', gazing upon his Lord for what he must have considered his last time, gave way to despair and threw himself into the sea with a great shout 'Yá Bahá'u'l-Abhá' [O Thou Glory of the Most Glorious]. He was rescued and condemned to continue to Cyprus with Mírzá Yaḥyá. Two years later he escaped, changed his name and went to 'Akká where he rejoined the companions of his Beloved. After the ascension of Bahá'u'lláh twenty-two years later, he went to live in Damascus and died there. He is immortalized in 'Abdu'l-Bahá's *Memorials of the Faithful*.

Chapter 16

'AKKÁ, THE MOST GREAT PRISON

MANY events taking place in the Holy Land today are associated with prophecies, predictions and promises in the Tannach, the Bible of the Jews, which is the Old Testament of the Christians and a Holy Book to the Muslims. Among the most spectacular of these has been the return of the Jews, prophesied in Deuteronomy 30, and largely dating from 1844, the year of the Báb's declaration and the Turkish Government's Edict of Toleration which assured protection from persecution to Jews and others in Ottoman domains.* This process led on to the Balfour Declaration and the establishment of the sovereign state of Israel in 1948. Since then the desert has blossomed like the rose under the skilled research and industry of Israeli agriculturalists and the beauties of Carmel are manifest at its very heart in the gardens and buildings of the Bahá'í World Centre.

Fulfilment of this ancient promise became the main theme of the Hebrew prophets, who painted wonderful pictures of a spiritually and materially transformed world.

I will give them one heart, and I will put a new spirit within you . . . that they may walk in my statutes . . . and they shall be my people, and I will be their God. (*Ezekiel 11:19–20*)

I will pour out my Spirit upon all flesh . . . (*Joel 2:28*)

---

* In 1867 the Turkish government permitted Jews to own real estate in Palestine.

I will put my law in their inward parts, and write it in their hearts; and will be their God, and they shall be my people. (*Jeremiah* 31:33)

The vile person shall be no more called liberal, nor the churl said to be bountiful. (*Isaiah* 32:5)

Righteousness and peace have kissed each other. (*Psalm* 85:10)

. . . the earth shall be full of the knowledge of the Lord, as the waters cover the sea. (*Isaiah* 11:9)

And the Lord shall be king over all the earth: in that day shall there be one Lord, and his name one. (*Zechariah* 14:9)

And he shall judge among many people, and rebuke strong nations afar off; and they shall beat their swords into plowshares, and their spears into pruning-hooks; nation shall not lift up sword against nation, neither shall they learn war any more. (*Micah* 4:3)

They identified this glorious outcome with the establishment on earth of the Kingdom of God through the appearance at the time of the end, in the Holy Land, of the World Redeemer, the Lord of Hosts. Isaiah, the greatest of them, had proclaimed: 'And it shall come to pass in the last days that . . . the Lord's house shall be established in the top of the mountains . . . and all nations shall flow unto it . . . let us go up to the mountain of the Lord, to the house of the God of Jacob; and he will teach us of his ways, and we will walk in his paths: for out of Zion shall go forth the law, and the word of the Lord from Jerusalem.' 'O Zion, that bringest good tidings; Get thee up into the high mountain; O Jerusalem, that bringest good tidings, lift up thy voice with strength; lift it up, be not afraid; say unto the cities of Judah: Behold your God! Behold the Lord God will come with strong hand, and his arm shall rule for him . . .' 'and the government shall be upon his shoulder: and his name shall be called Wonderful, Counsellor, The mighty God, The Everlasting Father, The Prince of Peace. Of the increase of his government and peace there shall be no end, upon the throne of David, and upon his kingdom, to order it, and to establish it with judgment and with justice from henceforth even for ever. The zeal of the Lord of hosts will perform this.'* David, in his Psalms, had predicted: 'Lift up your heads, O ye gates; even lift them up, ye everlasting doors; and the King of Glory shall come in. Who is this King of Glory? The Lord of Hosts, He is the King of Glory.' Amos foretold: 'The Lord will roar from Zion, and utter His voice from Jerusalem; and the habitations of the shepherds shall mourn, and the top of Carmel shall wither.'¹

Particular references to 'Akká are cited by Shoghi Effendi in *God Passes By*:

'Akká, itself, flanked by the 'glory of Lebanon', and lying in full view of the 'splendour of Carmel', at the foot of the hills which enclose the home of Jesus Christ Himself, had been described by David as 'the Strong City', designated by Hosea as 'a door of hope', and alluded to by Ezekiel as 'the gate that looketh towards the East', whereunto 'the glory of the God of Israel came from the way of the East', His voice 'like a noise of many waters'. To it the Arabian Prophet had referred as 'a city in Syria to which God hath shown His special mercy', situated 'betwixt two mountains . . . in the middle of a meadow', 'by the shore of the sea . . . suspended beneath the Throne', 'white, whose whiteness is pleasing unto God'. 'Blessed the man . . . that hath visited 'Akká, and blessed he that hath visited the visitor of 'Akká' . . . 'He that raiseth therein the call to prayer, his voice will be lifted up unto Paradise.' And again: 'The poor of 'Akká are the kings of Paradise and the princes thereof. A month in 'Akká is better than a thousand years elsewhere.' Moreover, in a remark-

---

* The late Archdeacon George Townshend commented on this passage in his book *Christ and Bahá'u'lláh*: 'To confirm orthodox Christian opinion it is customary in all churches to read on Christmas morning, as if it referred to Jesus, the passage which Isaiah wrote about the Lord of Hosts (Isaiah 9:6–7). Yet the descriptive titles given do not belong exclusively to Christ, while some of them He specifically repudiated as if to make such a mistaken reference to Himself impossible. He disclaimed being the Mighty God when He called Himself 'the Son of God' (John 5:18–47 where Jesus repudiates the charge that He claimed equality with God), disclaimed being the Father when He said, 'my Father is greater than I' (John 14:28); and being the Prince of Peace when He said, 'I came not to send peace, but a sword' (Matt. 10:34). He disclaimed bearing the government upon His shoulder or that it would be His judgement and justice forever when He said, 'My kingdom is not of this world' (John 18:36).

able tradition . . . which is recognized as an authentic utterance of Muḥammad, and is quoted by Mírzá Abu'l-Faḍl in his 'Fará'id', this significant prediction has been made: All of them [the companions of the Qá'im] shall be slain except One Who shall reach the plain of 'Akká, the Banquet-Hall of God.'[2]

When Bahá'u'lláh arrived at 'Akká in 1868 it was a decrepit, flea-infested, insanitary penal colony of the Turkish empire. So foul was the air that it was said that a bird flying over it would fall dead. The ancient Ptolemais, claiming, with others, to be the oldest city on earth, it became famous during the Crusades as St Jean d'Acre, for a time the headquarters of Richard the Lionheart. It has been laid waste more than once in its chequered history as it lay in the path of conflicting empires. In modern times it withstood Napoleon and frustrated his grandiose plan to march to India. Today it is a thriving, expanding city, a centre of tourism and point of Bahá'í pilgrimage.

Following the incident in Alexandria, described in the previous chapter, the ship to which the exiles had been transferred made for Haifa where they disembarked for a few hours. At that time Haifa was little more than a fishing village and the colony of German Templers who had gone there about 1868 to welcome the Messiah as He descended from the clouds. Many of their homes still bear texts engraved over their entrances. One of these is 'Der Herr ist Nahe' – the Lord is near.

In the late afternoon Bahá'u'lláh and His companions were taken aboard a sailing vessel to cross the bay to 'Akká. It was late August when the atmosphere of that part of Israel resembles a Turkish bath. There was no wind and the ship took eight hours to travel the short distance. Exposed to the pitiless sun and with no comforts the exiles suffered from the heat and humidity and confinement as greatly as they had from cold and exposure on two previous occasions.

Arrived at 'Akká there was no landing stage to the sea gate and the men had to wade ashore. It was proposed that the women and children should be carried on the men's backs, but 'Abdu'l-Bahá intervened and insisted on their being carried one by one in a chair which was made available by His efforts. So exhausted were they by that fearful crossing that Bahá'u'lláh's eldest daughter, Bahíyyih Khánum, the greatest woman of the Bahá'í Dispensation, was overcome and fainted.

The welcome accorded the little band was such as to strike terror into the stoutest heart. It had been proclaimed throughout the city, whose population was used to receiving the murderers and worst criminals of the Turkish empire, that these prisoners were the most debased and ineducable trouble-makers, deserving the severest punishment. Large numbers had gathered at the landing point to jeer at and threaten them and to see the 'God of the Persians', as they styled Bahá'u'lláh. The exhausted men, women and children were conducted through these callous, contemptuous crowds to the great bastion of the army barracks, fortified by moats and mighty ramparts.

But even in these desperate circumstances the grandeur and exaltation of Bahá'u'lláh could not be entirely hidden, and one or two of the less hardened, or more perceptive, of that hostile crowd, gazing upon His tragedy-laden but unperturbed countenance and witnessing the calm majesty of His demeanour, received an intimation of the hidden glory that was His, but which He would not use to compel the reverence and submission due to His station.

Adib Taherzadeh mentions two such individuals.* One was an old man who told the people of 'Akká that he saw in the face of Bahá'u'lláh 'signs of greatness and of majesty and of truthfulness' and that they should thank God for having sent them so great a personage. He also prophesied that great benefits would come to them and their city through Him, a truth which they later gratefully realized. Another man in the crowd sensed the radiance and power which emanated from Bahá'u'lláh and felt irresistibly drawn to Him. He later

* Taherzadeh. *The Revelation of Bahá'u'lláh*, vol. 3. Oxford: George Ronald, 1983.

became a Bahá'í and his daughter, who was born on the day that Bahá'u'lláh arrived in 'Akká, married our old friend Áshchí, the boy who had grown up among the exiled companions of Bahá'u'lláh and had become His cook.

The arrival of Bahá'u'lláh in 'Akká, although initiating the grimmest and most distressful period of His ministry, signalled the consummation of His mission and the dawning of that golden age when the purpose of man's life on the planet, as shaped and controlled by God, would be fulfilled. Mankind was approaching its majority and the revelation of God to man had, consonantly, reached its climax with the announcement of God's Kingdom on earth. After a period of utter confusion and chaos, inevitably associated with 'coming of age', a new era of unimaginable felicity and blessedness extending into the far reaches of unreckoned time would witness during the maturity of the human race the efflorescence and display of all those 'gems of divine virtue' hidden until now in the mine of man and reflecting the supernal splendour of that unseen spiritual realm which it will objectify. This vast and ever-advancing civilization will be sustained and vitalized by successive appearances of the Manifestation of God, who will offer new challenges and reveal ever more glorious heights to which the spirit of man may aspire as it progresses in the full splendour of its station as the beloved of God and the ultimate purpose of His creation.

Bahá'u'lláh Himself had testified, in a prophetic utterance made in the early days of His banishment to Adrianople, to the inner and outer import of His arrival at 'Akká:

Upon our arrival We were welcomed with banners of light, whereupon the Voice of the Spirit cried out saying: 'Soon will all that dwell on earth be enlisted under these banners.'[3]

Yet, of the outward circumstances of that critical time He wrote:

Know thou that upon Our arrival at this Spot, We chose to designate it as the 'Most Great Prison'. Though previously subjected in another land to chains and fetters, We yet refused to call it by that name. Say: Ponder thereon, O ye endued with understanding.[4]

The beginning of their exile in the Most Great Prison offered no encouragement whatever to the little company. The barracks, although spacious, were bare and filthy. For the first night Bahá'u'lláh was assigned to a room utterly devoid of furnishings of any kind. He was later moved to another room in which the plaster from the ceiling fell to the earth covering the floor. The rest of the company were hustled into another room whose floor was covered with mud. No food or water were provided and the cries of the children and general distress went unheeded by the ten soldiers allotted to guard them. 'Abdu'l-Bahá appealed to the guards to show mercy, and even sent a message to the Governor, but to no avail.

Later the Governor of the city came to inspect the situation and was so impressed by the bearing and leadership of 'Abdu'l-Bahá that he at once realized that his prisoners were not the desperate criminals described in the official documents and that Bahá'u'lláh and His family were of noble background. He made some mitigation of the inhuman conditions visited upon the exiles.

On the third day after His arrival, the Edict of the Sultán condemning Bahá'u'lláh to 'imprisonment for ever' was publicly read in the chief mosque of the city. The friends were stigmatized as criminals and corrupters of morals who were to be strictly confined and not to be allowed to associate with anyone.

Next morning, according to Áqá Ridá, another old friend of the Baghdad and Adrianople days, 'officials came to see what was happening to us'. Bahá'u'lláh spoke to them in tones of such wisdom and dignity that they were immediately disillusioned of the wild and malicious lies which had been circulated. One of them went so far as to say that such pure and sanctified souls had never before been seen in 'Akká.

Thus began once again the mysterious working of that divine power which had always aroused the glowing admiration, friendship and deep love of those who came under its influence. The fierce and independent Kurds had succumbed to its charm, the Bábí community in Baghdad and throughout Persia had responded wholeheartedly to its regenerative influence, while princes, governors of provinces and the lowliest of mankind had basked in its warmth; whole populations of cities had gathered to deplore the departure from their midst of the One from whom it radiated, and in Adrianople the consuls of European powers and the high officials of the region did their utmost to shield Him from the implacable hatred of His enemies. The little band of His fellow exiles, numbering sixty-six, who entered with Him the Most Great Prison, had more than once shown their preference for death rather than face separation from Him. Now it will be seen how from this mighty fortress He would defeat the two greatest despots of the time, complete the mission with which He had been entrusted, emerge at His own will from the 'everlasting imprisonment', become the cynosure of all hearts in the region of the Holy Land, and spread His fame abroad to such an extent that a scholar who would become one of the most distinguished orientalists of his time would come from the West to visit Him and have his account of that interview published by one of the oldest and most famous universities. His revelation of the new age and the provisions for its governance would plunge the world into confusion and chaos which only He could resolve.

The world's equilibrium hath been upset through the vibrating influence of this most great, this new World Order. Mankind's ordered life hath been revolutionized through the agency of this unique, this wondrous System – the like of which mortal eyes have never witnessed.[5]

The Hand of Omnipotence hath established His Revelation upon an unassailable, an enduring foundation. Storms of human strife are powerless to undermine its basis, nor will men's fanciful theories succeed in damaging its structure.[6]

The insanitary conditions in the prison, allied to the exhaustion of the friends and the inadequate nourishment provided, quickly took their toll. All but two fell sick and dysentery and malaria raged among them. No doctor attended nor were any medicaments provided. 'Abdu'l-Bahá, with the help of the one other member still on his feet, nursed and cared for the sufferers. Three succumbed including two brothers who died locked in each other's arms. Bahá'u'lláh gave His prayer rug to be sold and gave the money to the guards, who had refused to bury the three without first being given the necessary expenses. They interred the three bodies in the clothes they wore, without washing or shrouding or providing coffins, although, as Bahá'u'lláh stated, they were given twice the sum adequate for proper burial.

After this Bahá'u'lláh revealed a prayer for healing and asked the prisoners to recite it frequently and sincerely. They did so and all recovered.

The malice of Bahá'u'lláh's enemies was demonstrated anew by the actions of that same ambassador of Persia to the Sublime Porte who had so greatly exerted himself to bring about Bahá'u'lláh's banishment from Baghdad, Constantinople and Adrianople to this final imprisonment in 'the most desolate of the cities of the world, the most unsightly of them in appearance, the most detestable in climate, and the foulest in water.'[7] Having succeeded in inducing Sultán 'Abdu'l-'Azíz and his ministers to impose the very harshest conditions and strictest segregation upon the exiles, he now, driven by burning hatred, set about ensuring that there should be no relaxation of these orders in the slightest degree. A year after Bahá'u'lláh's banishment to 'Akká the ambassador, Hírzá Husayn Khán, reported to Teheran that he had issued instructions which forbade Bahá'u'lláh to associate with anyone except His family or to leave the house in which He was imprisoned for any reason whatsoever; he had sent the Consul-General in Damascus to 'Akká where he was to confer with the Governor about the strict maintenance of the exiles' imprisonment and to appoint a local representative to ensure that all the orders from the Sublime Porte were obeyed; the Consul himself was to visit 'Akká every three months to observe personally that there was no relaxation in the treatment of the prisoners and to report back to the Persian legation. One wonders with what authority a Persian diplomat could issue such instructions about Turkish citizens in Turkish territory.

But Mírza Husayn Khán's attitude to Bahá'u'lláh underwent a remarkable change. He later became a Grand Vizier of Persia and publicly stated that his government had made a gross error in banishing Bahá'u'lláh. He testified, 'With the power of two states, with the political planning of two governments, I tried to withstand Bahá'u'lláh and to contend with Him; the more I tried, the greater became His power and authority.' 'I came to realize that the powers of this world are unable to withstand this Cause.' Bahá'u'lláh Himself declared in *Epistle to the Son of the Wolf* that although what Mírzá Husayn Khán did 'was not actuated by his friendship', yet he was not dishonest but truly believed he was serving his country. 'As he was faithful, however, in the discharge of his duty, he deserveth Our commendation.' And in a letter to an individual believer He envisioned his forgiveness. Such was the justice and magnanimity of the Lord of mankind.

The isolation imposed on the exiles at the beginning of their imprisonment in 'Akká was so strict that the Bahá'ís in Persia could obtain no news of them. A rumour set afloat by Bahá'u'lláh's enemies to the effect that He had been drowned caused them such consternation that they approached the British telegraph office in Julfá with a request to ascertain the truth.

The window of Bahá'u'lláh's cell, heavily barred, gave upon the wall of the prison, two moats, the ramparts of the sea wall and beyond that the open sea. Pilgrims from Persia came, many on foot, hoping to elude the strict ban enforced by the Sultan's edict. Those who managed to reach the prison gates, within the city walls, were happy to content themselves with a brief glimpse of the face of their Beloved, seen in His cell from beyond the second moat. Those unable to enter the city waited beyond the third moat on the north side of the prison, and felt equally rewarded by a wave of His hand from a window giving on that aspect. Some had to return without even this consolation. One devoted soul managed to reach the bank of the moat whence he gazed 'for hours in rapt adoration at the window of his Beloved' only to fail to discern His face because of the weakness of his sight. He returned to the cave on Mount Carmel in which he had made his dwelling. Members of Bahá'u'lláh's family who watched this pitiful episode from another window were moved to tears. The great Nabíl, freed from imprisonment in Alexandria, managed to penetrate to the moat and succeeded in obtaining a glimpse of Bahá'u'lláh, but was recognized and had to flee the city. He 'continued to roam the countryside around Nazareth, Haifa, Jerusalem and Hebron, until the gradual relaxation of restrictions enabled him to rejoin the exiles'.[8]

Now occurred a tragedy which brought grief to the heart of Bahá'u'lláh and to His companions. Mírzá Mihdí, 'Abdu'l-Bahá's younger brother, a youth of twenty-two, while pacing the roof of the barracks during his evening devotions, fell through a skylight onto a wooden crate which pierced his ribs. Twenty-two hours later he died, supplicating his beloved Father to accept his life as a ransom for all those believers who were prevented from attaining His presence. He was an example of nobility and piety and meekness, and is known as the Purest Branch. Bahá'u'lláh revealed a prayer in his memory in which He wrote:

I have, O my Lord, offered up that which Thou hast given Me, that Thy servants may be quickened, and all that dwell on earth be united.[9]

And He addressed His son:

Thou art the Trust of God and His treasure in this Land. Erelong will God reveal through thee that which He hath desired.[10]

The death of the Purest Branch occurred on June 23rd, 1870, one year and ten months after the exiles entered the prison. The change in circumstances of the prisoners during this time was evident from the manner of his funeral. A tent was pitched in the middle of the barracks and on a table within it the body was washed and shrouded and placed in a new casket by members of the community, while 'Abdu'l-Bahá, in deep sorrow, paced outside the tent. The coffin was borne outside the city walls, escorted by fourteen guards and laid to rest next to the Shrine of Ṣáliḥ, a Prophet mentioned in Genesis* and the Qur'án. Seventy years later, the Guardian of the Faith would reinter the remains of the Purest Branch and his saintly mother Navváb in the Monument Gardens on Mount Carmel, within the shadow of the Shrine of the Báb.

Four months after this tragic event the Ottoman government required the barracks for a mobilization of the army, and Bahá'u'lláh and His company came out of the barracks to conditions of greater comfort and freedom. They were moved from house to house for a time, but eventually were assigned the house of 'Údí Khammár, which was attached to the house of 'Abbúd: when the partition was later removed the whole building became known as the house of 'Abbud and it was here that Bahá'u'lláh spent His remaining years within the city of 'Akká, before removing to the countryside in 1877, nine years after He had been sentenced to imprisonment for ever. Other houses were found for some of the exiles while some were consigned to a caravanserai near the sea walls.

Hardly had this mitigation of their sufferings been accomplished and their guards dismissed, when a crisis of catastrophic proportions engulfed the whole community, including Bahá'u'lláh Himself, and threatened to utterly reverse all the improvement in its standing which had so remarkably taken place.

It will be remembered that when the exiles were embarked

---

* See Gen. 10:24, 11:12–15.

upon their final banishment, Siyyid Muḥammad and Áqá Ján Big, the bitter enemies of Bahá'u'lláh and source of all the calumnies and misrepresentations to the authorities, were kept among the company of true companions sent to 'Akká, while four devoted believers were forced to accompany Mírzá Yaḥyá and his accomplices to Cyprus. These two miscreants lost no time in separating themselves from Bahá'u'lláh's followers and within three days of their arrival in the barracks persuaded the authorities to remove them to a room overlooking the land gate of the city. Here they began at once their insidious campaign of lies and invective against the companions and Bahá'u'lláh Himself, and ingratiated themselves with the guards by keeping watch on all who entered the land gate and identifying any whom they recognized as Bahá'ís, obviously seeking to attain the presence of Bahá'u'lláh or at least catch a glimpse of Him. While this latter activity caused untold grief to those hardy pilgrims who were caught and turned back at the very moment when it seemed they were about to attain their hearts' desire, the vilification of the prisoners had no effect on those officers who actually came into contact with them and began to realize the truth. But it did serve to confirm among the populace the prejudice implanted in them by the wild calumnies with which they had been regaled before the arrival of the exiles.

During the two years and two months of confinement in the barracks the two processes of gradual relaxation of the worst restrictions on the prisoners due to the growing respect of the authorities, and the inflammatory effect on the populace of Siyyid Muḥammad's campaign of calumny and abuse, continued simultaneously.

Towards the end of this period, Bahá'u'lláh, who had throughout His ministry constantly held before the friends, and urged them to maintain, the high standards of conduct to which the religion of God had always called the faithful and which are set out in clear detail in His own revelation, expelled from the community two people whose conduct was so

shameful as to damage severely the growing good name of the
Faith. Siyyid Muḥammad took immediate advantage of this
event, recruited them to himself and launched an even fiercer
campaign of 'abuse, calumny and intrigue . . . calculated to
arouse an already prejudiced and suspicious populace to a new
pitch of animosity and excitement'.[11] With the new freedom
of the friends to walk about the city, the situation was
explosive as they were subjected to abuse and threatened with
violence in the streets and their children were pursued and
pelted with stones. The life of Bahá'u'lláh was in danger.
Constantly and emphatically He had always forbidden retaliation
against persecutors and at this critical moment He sent back to
Beirut an Arab believer who found himself unable to conform
to this strict command. But alas, seven of the companions
attacked and killed three of their tormentors, including Siyyid
Muḥammad and Áqá Ján Big.

The scene of this crime was the room over the land gate
occupied by Siyyid Muḥammad. H. M. Balyuzi writes, 'The
sound of pistol shots, and of shouts and yelling, brought Sáliḥ
Páshá [the Governor], from his house. And then pandemonium
broke out.'[12] 'Akká was in uproar. Áqá Riḍá recorded: 'All,
young and old, notables and humble folk, the Governor, the
Chief of Police, and troops rose up, as if a powerful state had
made an attack on them. Armed with stones and sticks,
swords and rifles they set out towards the house of the Blessed
Perfection* and the houses of the companions, arresting
whomever they met.'[13] That evening a steamer anchored at
'Akká and all communication with it was immediately
banned.

Two officials entered Bahá'u'lláh's house and were met by
'Abdu'l-Bahá and three of the companions, whom they
requested to accompany them to Government House. When
they asked that Bahá'u'lláh should come too, 'Abdu'l-Bahá
went to His room and presented their request. He came out

---

* One of the many titles by which the early believers referred to Bahá'u'lláh.

and they all walked to the Seraye, followed by the crowd and those companions not yet arrested. Áqá Riḍá states that everyone who saw Him on that walk 'marvelled at the power emanating from His person', and one of the inhabitants of 'Ákká, seeing Him, instantly believed in Him and joined the ranks of the companions.

One of those present as Bahá'u'lláh entered the Seraye records that the Governor, the Chief of Police, the Chief Secretary and other officials stood up as He walked to the top of the room and took a seat. 'There was utter silence until, at last, the commandant of the garrison spoke:

"Is it meet that your men should commit such a heinous deed?" '[14]

Bahá'u'lláh replied: 'If one of your soldiers were to commit a reprehensible act, would you be held responsible, and be punished in his place?'[15]

Again there was total silence until, according to Áqá Riḍá, Bahá'u'lláh rose and went into another room. He was lodged that night in a room of a caravanserai, and Mírzá Áqá Ján was allowed to go to His house and bring what He needed for the night. He was transferred for the next two nights to better quarters in the same neighbourhood.

Shoghi Effendi relates that ''Abdu'l-Bahá was thrown into prison and chained during the first night, after which He was permitted to join His Father. Twenty-five of the companions were cast into another prison and shackled, all of whom, except those responsible for that odious deed, whose imprisonment lasted several years, were, after six days, moved to the Khán-i-Shávirdí, and there placed, for six months, under confinement'.[16]

On the third day Bahá'u'lláh was again led to the Governor's office. That official had, meantime, cabled a full report to the Válí (Governor) of Syria in Damascus who reprimanded him for his treatment of Bahá'u'lláh. Shoghi Effendi relates, from an account of an observer present at the interview which took place: 'When interrogated, He was asked to state His name and that of the country from which He came. "It is more manifest than the sun," He answered. The same question was put to Him again, to which He gave the following reply: "I deem it not proper to mention it. Refer to the farmán of the government which is in your possession." Once again they, with marked deference, reiterated their request, whereupon Bahá'u'lláh spoke with majesty and power these words: "My name is Bahá'u'lláh [Light of God], and My country is Núr [Light]. Be ye apprized of it." Turning then, to the Muftí, He addressed him words of veiled rebuke, after which He spoke to the entire gathering, in such vehement and exalted language that none made bold to answer Him. Having quoted verses from the Súriy-i-Mulúk [Tablet to the Kings], He, afterwards, arose and left the gathering. The Governor, soon after, sent word that He was at liberty to return to His home, and apologized for what had occurred.'[17]

The distress caused to Bahá'u'lláh by this episode was immeasurable. He lamented,

My captivity cannot harm Me. That which can harm Me is the conduct of those who love Me, who claim to be related to Me, and yet perpetrate what causeth My heart and My pen to groan.

My captivity can bring on Me no shame. Nay, by My life, it conferreth on Me glory. That which çan make Me ashamed is the conduct of such of My followers as profess to love Me, yet in fact follow the Evil One.[18]

The humiliating and dangerous situation thus created was endured for a time and then began 'a transformation in the fortunes of the Faith even more conspicuous than the revolutionary change effected during the latter years of Bahá'u'lláh's sojourn in Baghdád'.[19]

The chief factors in this remarkable change were the majesty and grandeur of Bahá'u'lláh, gradually becoming evident to the public as it heard about Him from those who had been overawed by being in His presence or had had to deal with Him; and, more immediately, the daily contact of 'Abdu'l-

Bahá with all sections of the population as He demonstrated through His constant devotion to their care and service that He was indeed the Perfect Exemplar of the Bahá'í teachings. Many years later the eminent Christian divine, the Reverend Canon Cheyne* would write of Him, 'No one, so far as my observation reaches, has lived the perfect life like 'Abdu'l-Bahá.'

'Abdu'l-Bahá's leadership of the Bahá'í community and His shielding of Bahá'u'lláh from the curiosity and invasion of those who would violate His privacy contributed greatly to the improvement in the status of the exiles and the Faith which they professed. The fall from power of those malicious officials further eased the situation and finally a new Governor of 'Akká was appointed, Ahmad Big Tawfíq.

This 'sagacious and humane governor' undeceived by the ploy of the antagonists in collecting the writings of Bahá'u'lláh, interpolating them and submitting them to the authorities as proof of Bahá'u'lláh's subversion, was, instead, deeply impressed by what he read and became eager to learn more. He reviewed the episode of the murders and released the innocent members of the community who had been confined to the Khán-i-Shávirdí. He was captivated by 'Abdu'l-Bahá and displayed publicly great reverence for Him, sending his son to Him for instruction. Such was his admiration for the author of those writings and for His illustrious son that it was said his favourite counsellors were those very exiles who were the followers of the prisoner in his custody. He made many requests for an interview with Bahá'u'lláh and when that bounty was finally granted he implored permission to render Him some service. Bahá'u'lláh suggested that he restore the aqueduct which had been built about 1815 to bring fresh water to 'Akká from the Kabrí Springs, some five miles north of the city, and which for thirty years had been broken down

---

* Distinguished 'higher critic' of the Bible and author of *The Reconciliation of Races and Religions*. He arranged 'Abdu'l-Bahá's visit to Oxford in 1912 and entertained Him and His party at his house.

and useless, with the disastrous consequences to the climate of 'Akká which so oppressed its inhabitants. The Governor set to work and it was that action which no doubt contributed to the belief soon current in 'Akká that its climate changed with the arrival of Bahá'u'lláh.

Ahmad Big Tawfíq remained Governor of the city for two years, during which time the transformation in the status of the Bahá'í community took place. Bahá'u'lláh was venerated and referred to by the populace as the 'august leader' or 'his highness'. The friends were able to establish shops and businesses and to move about with freedom. These remissions of the Sultan's intent had all emanated from the Governor himself and his officers; no petition or complaints had been made by the Bahá'ís. But when Ahmad Big Tawfíq was called to another post a grand farewell was arranged for him by the Bahá'ís. 'Abdu'l-Bahá had a tent set up in an open space near the house of 'Abbúd, where he could receive the guests and all those who wished to say goodbye. Meals were provided to everyone who came. This hospitality greatly astonished the people, to whom it was explained that if such expression of gratitude had been made while the Governor was in power it might well have been misconstrued; now it could be offered freely. The Governor continued to the last moment to express his sorrow at his separation from Bahá'u'lláh and His beloved son.

It was during Ahmad Big Tawfíq's governorship that Bahá'u'lláh, in 1873, revealed the *Kitáb-i-Aqdas*, the Most Holy Book of the Bahá'í Dispensation, the repository of the laws and ordinances which were to sustain His future world order, in which the institutions of that same order are established, the function of interpretation of His revelation and the succession to the headship of His Faith ordained. In it are contained His messages to those rulers and monarchs not addressed in individual letters, and the assurance of continual guidance to mankind through the provision of His Covenant.

Shoghi Effendi, Bahá'u'lláh's great-grandson and Guardian

of the Bahá'í Faith, has described this book as 'the principal repository of that Law which the Prophet Isaiah had anticipated, and which the writer of the Apocalypse had described as the "new heaven" and the "new earth", as "the Tabernacle of God", as the "Holy City", as the "Bride", the "New Jerusalem coming down from God", this "Most Holy Book", whose provisions must remain inviolate for no less than a thousand years, and whose system will embrace the entire planet, may well be regarded as the brightest emanation of the mind of Bahá'u'lláh, as the Mother Book of His Dispensation, and the Charter of His New World Order.'[20]

With the exception of one, successive Governors of 'Akká continued the benevolent policy towards the exiles first practised by Aḥmad Big Tawfíq. The one exception was his immediate successor, a two-faced man who tried to reverse the growing ascendancy of the Bahá'í community but who came to grief as a result of his duplicity. On assuming office he was all friendliness and respect outwardly, but was secretly conspiring with the few remaining enemies of Bahá'u'lláh in 'Akká. Together they launched another campaign to the higher authorities of the province, complaining in constant reports that these degenerate exiles who had been sent to 'Akká by order of the Sultan to be segregated lest they corrupt others now enjoyed freedom to go about as they pleased and even to operate lucrative shops and businesses. An order came from Damascus that since the Bahá'ís were prisoners they had no right to keep shops and engage in business. The new Governor was delighted and planned a dramatic triumph for himself. It was Ramadan, the Muslim month of fasting, so he planned to march into the bazaar with his attendants and order the Bahá'ís to shut down and abandon their shops and offices, a public act which would be disastrous to the standing of the Bahá'í community.

Bahá'u'lláh became aware of this plan and commanded the friends to close their shops and stay away from them. On the day, the Governor, attended by his staff and the enemies of the Faith entered the bazaar with great 'pomp and circumstance' only to find the Bahá'í shops closed. He commented that it was Ramadan and a little early and the offenders were certain to appear before long; he would wait in the sentry's house. After an hour or so the Muftí of 'Akká arrived, somewhat concerned and bearing a sheet of paper which he handed to the Governor. It was a cable from the Válí (governor of a province) in Damascus, dismissing the Governor and appointing the Muftí as his temporary replacement. The Válí also requested that his greetings be conveyed to His Eminence 'Abbás Effendi ('Abdu'l-Bahá's formal name and title as head of a religious community).

This foray by the implacable enemies in 'Akká was the last concerted effort they were to make during the earthly life of Bahá'u'lláh, although 'Abdu'l-Bahá, His appointed successor and Centre of His Covenant, became the focus of their hatred and had to withstand their constant harassment and efforts to destroy Him, while persecution and oppression of the Faith in Persia continue until this day.

Following the revelation in 1873 of the *Kitáb-i-Aqdas*, 'the most signal act of His ministry', the remaining four years of the nine which comprised Bahá'u'lláh's confinement in the prison-city witnessed a stream of writings, reaffirming, clarifying, categorizing the principles and fundamental tenets of His Faith, elucidating and supplementing the provisions of the *Kitáb-i-Aqdas*, urging mankind to 'consort with all men in a spirit of friendliness and fellowship', to promote the unity of the human race, 'the monarch of all aspirations', to recognize justice as the 'standard bearer of love and bounty' upon which depend 'the organization of the world and the tranquillity of mankind' and setting forth an entire philosophy of the universe and the precepts, attitudes and values of a new world civilization.[21] During the whole of His ministry prayers and meditations poured from His pen for the education, refinement and spiritualization of mankind.

Throughout His sojourn in the prison city we have seen Bahá'u'lláh surmount the appalling conditions of His captivity,

become the comforter of a hapless and helpless yet blessed
company, the focal point of the hopes and longings of
thousands left in those countries through which He had
passed, revealing in increasing measure the power and majesty
of His station. Even the members of His family knew Him
first as their Lord and were reverent and submissive before
Him. When He sat by the death bed of the Purest Branch,
that saintly youth was beatified and exalted beyond any
condition which an earthly father could induce. Navváb was so
overwhelmed with grief at the loss of her second son amidst
such tragic circumstances that she wept uncontrollably and
could not be consoled. Bahá'u'lláh assured her that God had
accepted the sacrifice of her son as a ransom for the opening of
the doors of pilgrimage and the quickening of all mankind.
Navváb's grief was assuaged and she became content with the
will of God.

Now after the long years of suffering, a period of peace and
honour ensued. Such was the veneration in which Bahá'u'lláh
was held that the population of 'Akká openly proclaimed their
pleasure with His presence among them. Despite the Sultan's
farmán, pilgrims were allowed and even assisted to enter the
city and one Governor even intimated that the prisoner was
free to go through its gates whenever He wished, an offer
which Bahá'u'lláh declined. 'Azíz Páshá, the Governor of
Adrianople who had become so devoted to Bahá'u'lláh and His
eldest son during their residence there, now a Válí, came twice
from Beirut to pay his respects. The Governor of 'Akká and a
European General, granted the unusual honour of an interview
with Bahá'u'lláh, evinced such reverence before Him that the
General 'remained kneeling on the ground near the door'.[22]*

* There is some evidence to suggest that this was General Gordon; research may
confirm it.

Chapter 17

FREEDOM

WHEN Bahá'u'lláh entered the prison he proclaimed, 'Fear not. These doors shall be opened, My tent shall be pitched on Mount Carmel, and the utmost joy shall be realized.'[1] Let 'Abdu'l-Bahá tell the story of how His beloved Father eventually left the city of His 'everlasting imprisonment'.

Bahá'u'lláh loved the beauty and verdure of the country. One day He passed the remark: 'I have not gazed on verdure for nine years. The country is the world of the soul, the city is the world of bodies.' When I heard indirectly of this saying I realized that He was longing for the country, and I was sure that whatever I could do towards the carrying out of His wish would be successful. There was in 'Akká at that time a man called Muhammad Páshá Safwat who was very much opposed to us. He had a palace called Mazra'ih, about four miles north of the city, a lovely place, surrounded by gardens and with a stream of running water. I went and called on this Páshá at his home. I said: 'Páshá, you have left the palace empty, and are living in 'Akká.' He replied: 'I am an invalid and cannot leave the city. If I go there it is lonely and I am cut off from my friends.' I said: 'While you are not living there and the place is empty, let it to us.' He was amazed at the proposal, but soon consented. I got the house at a very low rent, about five pounds per annum, paid him for five years and made a contract. I sent labourers to repair the place and put the garden in order and had a bath built. I also had a carriage prepared for the use of the Blessed Beauty. One day I determined to go and see the place for myself. Notwithstanding the repeated injunctions given in successive firmans that we were on no account to pass the limits of the city walls, I walked out through the City Gate. Gendarmes were on guard, but they made no objection, so I proceeded straight to the palace. The next day I again went out, with some friends and officials, unmolested and unopposed, although the guards and sentinels stood on both sides of the city gates. Another day I arranged a banquet, spread a table under the pine trees of Bahjí, and gathered round it the notables and officials of the town. In the evening we all returned to the town together.

One day I went to the Holy Presence of the Blessed Beauty and said: 'The palace at Mazra'ih is ready for You, and a carriage to drive You there.' (At that time there were no carriages in 'Akká or Haifa.) He refused to go, saying: 'I am a prisoner.' Later I requested Him again, but got the same answer. I went so far as to ask Him a third time, but He still said 'No!' and I did not dare to insist further. There was, however, in 'Akká a certain Muhammadan Shaykh, a well-known man with considerable influence,* who loved Bahá'u'lláh and was greatly favoured by Him. I called this Shaykh and explained the position to him. I said, 'You are daring. Go tonight to His Holy Presence, fall on your knees before Him, take hold of His hands and do not let go until He promises to leave the city!' He was an Arab . . . He went directly to Bahá'u'lláh and sat down close to His knees. He took hold of the hands of the Blessed Beauty and kissed them and asked: 'Why do you not leave the city?' He said: 'I am a prisoner.' The Shaykh replied: 'God forbid! Who has the power to make you a prisoner? You have kept yourself in prison. It was your own will to be imprisoned, and now I beg you to come out and go to the palace. It is beautiful and verdant. The trees are lovely, and the oranges like balls of fire!' As often as the Blessed Beauty said: 'I am a prisoner, it cannot be,' the Shaykh took His hands and kissed them. For a whole hour he kept on pleading. At last Bahá'u'lláh said, 'Khaylí khúb (very good)' and the Shaykh's patience and persistence were rewarded . . . In spite of the strict firman of 'Abdu'l-Azíz which prohibited my meeting or having any intercourse with the Blessed Perfection, I took the carriage the next day and drove with Him to the palace. No one made any objection. I left Him there and returned myself to the city.[2]

* He was the Muftí.

Chapter 18

BAHJÍ – THE FINAL YEARS

THE constantly changing pattern of Bahá'u'lláh's earthly life had now come full circle. Born to wealth and high estate, He had passed through the nadir of abasement and despoliation; imprisoned, chained, tortured, vilified, four times exiled, in His final years He achieved an ascendancy and manifested a majesty which no earthly power could resemble. All who had opposed Him were swept away or reduced to ignominy. The efforts of two despotic emperors, their powerful ministers and a host of fanatical Muslim divines to destroy Him and the Faith which He proclaimed, were utterly frustrated and became the cause of His success. He Himself commented:

The Ottoman Sultán, without any justification, or reason, arose to oppress Us, and sent Us to the fortress of 'Akká. His imperial farmán decreed that none should associate with Us, and that We should become the object of the hatred of every one. The Hand of Divine power, therefore, swiftly avenged Us. It first loosed the winds of destruction upon his two irreplaceable ministers and confidants, 'Alí and Fu'ád, after which that Hand was stretched out to roll up the panoply of 'Azíz himself, and to seize him, as He only can seize, Who is the Mighty, the Strong.[1]

While 'Abdu'l-Bahá testified:

His enemies intended that His imprisonment should completely destroy and annihilate the blessed Cause, but this prison was, in reality, of the greatest assistance, and became the means of its development . . . This illustrious Being uplifted His Cause in the Most Great Prison. From this Prison His light was shed abroad; His fame conquered the world, and the proclamation of His glory reached the East and the West . . . Until our time no such thing has ever occurred.[2]

. . . the doors of majesty and true sovereignty were flung wide open . . . The rulers of Palestine envied His influence and power. Governors and mutisarrifs, generals and local officials, would humbly request the honour of attaining His presence – a request to which He seldom acceded.[3]

Mazra'ih, the property which 'Abdu'l-Bahá had secured for His Father, was indeed a delightful place. During the British mandate between the two world wars, it was occupied by General McNeill, whose wife, together with her childhood playmate and life-long friend Queen Marie of Romania, were devoted to Bahá'u'lláh and His teachings. It is now maintained with loving care by the Bahá'í Faith, whose pilgrims enjoy visiting it. For two years Bahá'u'lláh remained there, frequently visiting the homes of the friends in 'Akká, including those of His two brothers who had been His staunch supporters and prominent members of the banished community from the very beginning in Iraq. There was also to the east of the city a small garden, called Na'mayn after the river in the midst of which it was situated. It contained a fountain and benches under its great mulberry tree and a small cottage suitable for overnight stays. Members of the community settled on and farmed the adjoining fields. Here the friends would attend Bahá'u'lláh and bask in the sunshine of His presence. Picnics were held which His granddaughters described as 'the greatest of our joys. . . . How happy we were with Him. He was indeed the brightness of our lives in that time of difficulty.'[4]

Many stories are told of Bahá'u'llah in this garden, which He referred to as 'Our verdant Isle' and which he named Ridván (Paradise). May Maxwell of immortal memory was a member of the first group of pilgrims from the West who in 1898 visited 'Abdu'l-Bahá in 'Akká when some of the restrictions had again been imposed. She visited the garden and recorded the following story told by Abu'l-Qásim, the gardener who devoted his life to maintaining in perfect order Bahá'u'lláh's favoured retreat. It seems that one hot summer there was a plague of locusts in the area and a cloud of them settled on the garden. Abu'l-Qásim ran to the cottage where Bahá'u'lláh was resting and besought Him, 'My Lord, the locusts have come and are eating away the shade from above Thy blessed head. I beg of Thee to cause them to depart.' Bahá'u'lláh smiled and said, 'The locusts must be fed; let them be.' Poor Abu'l-Qásim went back to watch the work of destruction and then, unable to bear it, went again to Bahá'u'lláh and implored Him to send the pests away. This time He arose and went and stood beneath the trees on which the swarms were feasting. Then He said, 'Abu'l-Qásim does not want you; God protect you,' and He shook the hem of His robe. All the locusts immediately rose in a body and flew away. Mrs Maxwell relates that at the end of his story Abu'l-Qásim exclaimed with strong emotion, 'Oh! blessed are these eyes to have seen such things; oh, blessed are these ears to have heard such things'; and she concludes, 'In parting he gave us flowers to show his love.'[5] Such stories from heavenly memories have no authority in the Bahá'í canon; they are called 'pilgrim's notes' and are treasured by Bahá'ís, coming from the lips of those who actually saw Bahá'u'lláh and served Him.

A truly authentic utterance, related to the Riḍván Garden, comes from Bahá'u'lláh Himself. More than once He indicated that divine revelation came to Him through 'a maiden' or a 'Maid of Heaven', and in the Tablets of *Ishráqát* and *Ṭarázát* which are concerned with the elements of good character, we find the following:

We will now mention unto thee Trustworthiness and the station thereof in the estimation of God, thy Lord, the Lord of the Mighty Throne. One day of days We repaired unto Our Green Island. Upon Our arrival, We beheld its streams flowing, and its trees luxuriant, and the sunlight playing in their midst. Turning Our face to the right, We beheld what the pen is powerless to describe; nor can it set forth that which the eye of the Lord of Mankind witnessed in that most sanctified, that most sublime, that blest, and most exalted Spot. Turning, then, to the left We gazed on one of the Beauties of the Most Sublime Paradise, standing on a pillar of light, and calling aloud saying: 'O inmates of earth and heaven! Behold ye My beauty, and My radiance, and My revelation, and My effulgence. By God, the True One! I am Trustworthiness and the revelation thereof, and the beauty thereof. I will recompense whosoever will cleave unto Me, and recognize My rank and station, and hold fast unto My hem. I am the most great ornament of the people of Bahá, and the vesture of glory unto all who are in the kingdom of creation. I am the supreme instrument for the prosperity of the world, and the horizon of assurance unto all beings.'

When Bahá'u'lláh was a prisoner in the barracks, a wealthy citizen of 'Akká, 'Údí Khammár by name, began to build for himself and his family a palatial country residence some two miles north of the city, which he occupied about 1871. During the early part of 1879, less than two years after Bahá'u'lláh left His confinement, an epidemic disease ravaged the area and many people fled in panic. 'Údí Khammár died and was buried near the wall of his palace, but his family fled and the place became vacant. 'Abdu'l-Bahá rented and later purchased it and Bahá'u'lláh moved into it in September 1879. There for the remaining thirteen years of His earthly life He lived, a majestic and venerated figure. Dr J. E. Esslemont, whom we have already invoked, has left this note:

Having in His earlier years of hardship shown how to glorify God in a state of poverty and ignominy, Bahá'u'lláh in His later years at Bahjí showed how to glorify God in a state of honour and affluence. The offerings of hundreds of thousands of devoted followers placed at His disposal large funds which He was called upon to administer. Although His life at Bahjí has been described as truly regal, in the highest sense of the word, yet it must not be imagined that it was characterized by material splendour or extravagance. The Blessed

Perfection and His family lived in very simple and modest fashion, and expenditure on selfish luxury was a thing unknown in that household. Near His home the believers prepared a beautiful garden called Ridván, in which He often spent many consecutive days or even weeks, sleeping at night in a little cottage in the garden. Occasionally He went further afield. He made several visits to 'Akká and Haifa, and on more than one occasion pitched His tent on Mount Carmel, as He had predicted when imprisoned in the barracks at 'Akká.[6]

The Mansion of Bahjí, as this palace is now known, was the scene of E. G. Browne's historic visit. In addition to those portions of his memoir already quoted, he has left us this brief description:

. . . with a throb of wonder and awe, I became definitely conscious that the room was not untenanted. In the corner where the divan met the wall sat a wondrous and venerable figure, crowned with a felt head-dress of the kind called *táj* by dervishes (but of unusual height and make), round the base of which was wound a small white turban.*

From Bahjí Bahá'u'lláh visited Mount Carmel three times and on each occasion pitched His tent there. These visits were in addition to the first one when the steamer carrying the exiles from Alexandria put in at Haifa and the whole company was taken ashore for several hours.

The first visit from the Mansion was in 1883, when He stayed for a few days in a home of one of the German Templers; the second occasion was in 1890 during which He stayed part of the time in a house in the German colony known as Oliphant house and His tent was pitched on a piece of land opposite. His final visit was in 1891 and lasted three months during which time He stayed in a house near the German colony with His tent pitched nearby.

It was during the last visit that two historic and portentous

---

* See Frontispiece for remainder of description.

events took place, the command to erect the Shrine of the Báb on a designated spot, and the revelation of the *Tablet of Carmel*.

One day, Bahá'u'lláh, standing with 'Abdu'l-Bahá in a grove of cypress trees about halfway up the slopes of the mountain, pointed to a spot immediately below and instructed the Master to inter there the remains of the Martyr-Herald of His Faith within a befitting mausoleum. The wonderful story of how these sacred remains were rescued from the moat outside the barrack walls of Tabríz, into which they had been thrown immediately after He and His immortal disciple had been shot, how they had been transferred from place to place until brought to the care of 'Abdu'l-Bahá in 'Akká, how the Master had discharged His mission and Shoghi Effendi had beautified the building erected by 'Abdu'l-Bahá and laid out the surrounding garden is related in detail by Shoghi Effendi in his monumental history *God Passes By*, by Nabíl in *The Dawn-Breakers*, by H. M. Balyuzi in his life of 'Abdu'l-Bahá, in volume four of Adib Taherzadeh's *The Revelation of Bahá'u'lláh* and in other accounts. Today the dominant feature of the Haifa scene is the golden-domed Shrine of the Báb, the Queen of Carmel, resting superb amidst its gardens and avenues, and even now its beauty being further enhanced by the construction of nineteen terraces, each with its fountains and gardens, nine from the foot of God's mountain to the tenth on which stands the magnificent Shrine itself, and nine from there to the summit.

The *Tablet of Carmel* was revealed on a day when Bahá'u'lláh had visited that part of the mountain close to the Cave of Elijah, over which the monks of the Carmelite Order have erected and maintain their monastery. It is said that it was built to welcome the Lord when He should return as promised. The monks saw Him but were veiled from Him as were the priests and leaders in His previous appearance nineteen hundred years ago.

The *Tablet of Carmel* is one of the three great charters by which the unfoldment of Bahá'u'lláh's World Order is guided.

Its form and style are distinctly characteristic of a great part of Bahá'u'lláh's revelation, and are apparent in the following translation by Shoghi Effendi:

All glory be to this Day, the Day in which the fragrances of mercy have been wafted over all created things, a Day so blest that past ages and centuries can never hope to rival it, a Day in which the countenance of the Ancient of Days hath turned towards His holy seat. Thereupon the voices of all created things, and beyond them those of the Concourse on high, were heard calling aloud: 'Haste thee, O Carmel, for lo, the light of the countenance of God, the Ruler of the Kingdom of Names and Fashioner of the heavens, hath been lifted upon thee.'

Seized with transports of joy, and raising high her voice, she thus exclaimed: 'May my life be a sacrifice to Thee, inasmuch as Thou hast fixed Thy gaze upon me, hast bestowed upon me Thy bounty, and hast directed towards me Thy steps. Separation from Thee, O Thou Source of everlasting life, hath well nigh consumed me, and my remoteness from Thy presence hath burned away my soul. All praise be to Thee for having enabled me to hearken to Thy call, for having honoured me with Thy footsteps, and for having quickened my soul through the vitalizing fragrance of Thy Day and the shrilling voice of Thy Pen, a voice Thou didst ordain as Thy trumpet-call amidst Thy people. And when the hour at which Thy resistless Faith was to be made manifest did strike, Thou didst breathe a breath of Thy spirit into Thy Pen, and lo, the entire creation shook to its very foundations, unveiling to mankind such mysteries as lay hidden within the treasuries of Him Who is the Possessor of all created things.'

No sooner had her voice reached that most exalted Spot than We made reply: 'Render thanks unto Thy Lord, O Carmel. The fire of thy separation from Me was fast consuming thee, when the ocean of My presence surged before thy face, cheering thine eyes and those of all creation, and filling with delight all things visible and invisible. Rejoice, for God hath in this Day established upon thee His throne, hath made thee the dawning-place of His signs and the day spring of the evidences of His Revelation. Well is it with him that circleth around thee, that proclaimeth the revelation of thy glory, and recounteth that which the bounty of the Lord thy God hath showered upon thee. Seize thou the Chalice of Immortality in the name of thy Lord, the All-Glorious, and give thanks unto Him, inasmuch as He, in token of His mercy unto thee, hath turned thy sorrow into gladness, and transmuted thy grief into blissful joy. He, verily, loveth the spot which hath been made the seat of His throne, which His footsteps have trodden, which hath been honoured by His presence, from which He raised His call, and upon which He shed His tears.

'Call out to Zion, O Carmel, and announce the joyful tidings: He that was hidden from mortal eyes is come! His all-conquering sovereignty is manifest; His all-encompassing splendour is revealed. Beware lest thou hesitate or halt. Hasten forth and circumambulate the City of God that hath descended from heaven, the celestial Kaaba round which have circled in adoration the favoured of God, the pure in heart, and the company of the most exalted angels. Oh, how I long to announce unto every spot on the surface of the earth, and to carry to each one of its cities, the glad-tidings of this Revelation — a Revelation to which the heart of Sinai hath been attracted, and in whose name the Burning Bush is calling: "Unto God, the Lord of Lords, belong the kingdoms of earth and heaven." Verily this is the Day in which both land and sea rejoice at this announcement, the Day for which have been laid up those things which God, through a bounty beyond the ken of mortal mind or heart, hath destined for revelation. Ere long will God sail His Ark upon thee, and will manifest the people of Bahá who have been mentioned in the Book of Names.'

Sanctified be the Lord of all mankind, at the mention of Whose name all the atoms of the earth have been made to vibrate, and the Tongue of Grandeur hath been moved to disclose that which had been wrapt in His knowledge and lay concealed within the treasury of His might. He, verily, through the potency of His name, the Mighty, the All-Powerful, the Most High, is the ruler of all that is in the heavens and all that is on earth.

The years of Bahá'u'lláh's residence in Bahjí were years of blissful delight for the Bahá'ís living in 'Akká, who had freedom to attend on Him and pursue their lives under the benevolent and firm leadership of 'Abdu'l-Bahá. They were years of intense activity for Bahá'u'lláh, from Whose Pen streamed innumerable verses, letters to individuals, prayers and exhortations, weighty Tablets supplementing the fundamentals of His World Order already revealed in the Most Holy Book (*Kitáb-i-Aqdas*), or reaffirming and elaborating some of the laws prescribed in that same book.

Particular mention must be made of the unique and impregnable Covenant of Bahá'u'lláh, whose provisions have maintained the unity of His Faith, preserved its sacred writings from misinterpretation and closed for ever the doors of sect and schism within the Bahá'í community. A number of misguided souls have tried to break that Covenant and assume leadership but none has succeeded; all attempts have failed dismally, broken on the inviolable rock of Bahá'u'lláh's clear and written appointment of His successor, His eldest son, 'Abdu'l-Bahá, the Most Great Branch. In the *Kitáb-i-Aqdas* and later in His Will Bahá'u'lláh named 'Abdu'l-Bahá Head of the Faith, Centre of the Covenant, sole Interpreter of the revelation and upon Him He conferred absolute authority, whatsoever He would decide having the same validity as the word of Bahá'u'lláh Himself. 'Abdu'l-Bahá perpetuated the Covenant through His own Will and Testament and the provisions of the *Kitáb-i-Aqdas*, so that today the Bahá'í world enjoys complete freedom for every individual to understand the revelation independently, but none may force his own view upon others. The administration of Bahá'u'lláh's World Order, even in its embryonic stage, is a vast and fascinating study, whose pursuit leads to ever closer and enduring unity.

The final book of Bahá'u'lláh's revelation is *Epistle to the Son of the Wolf*, written in 1891 within a year of His death. It is addressed to Shaykh Muḥammad-Taqí, who emulated his father in torturing and murdering Bahá'ís in Persia. It begins with a powerful exhortation to this wicked man to repent and to beg God's forgiveness. In the course of a long prayer which he is urged to offer, his acts of bestial cruelty are enumerated and the manner of his supplication stated, but nowhere is there any hint of revenge or retaliation. His deeds are condemned but with the hope that he will change his ways. Even to this bitterest enemy Bahá'u'lláh offers only reforming counsels and reveals the compassion and limitless love which He has for all mankind.

The remainder of this epistle is a recapitulation for the Shaykh of Bahá'u'lláh's message to mankind. Frequently quoting His own previous writings, He offers a new way of life and a new set of values and a new knowledge of himself to this misguided man.

What vision inspired 'Údí Khammár to inscribe over the entrance to his palace the following message which in translation reads: 'Greetings and salutation rest upon this mansion which increaseth in splendour through the passage of time. Manifold wonders and marvels are found therein, and pens are baffled in attempting to describe them.'

Bahjí, which means 'delight', has indeed increased in splendour and become a place of heavenly peace, of blissful contemplation and quiet repose. Its ancillary buildings have been brought into harmony with the extensive park, comprising flower gardens, lawns and tree-lined avenues, walks and groves of pine and eucalyptus, which extends in a vast circle circumscribing the entire area. At its heart lies the holiest spot on earth, the Shrine in which is interred the mortal frame of that Great One from God, the Lord of Hosts, the King of Kings, the Judge, the Lawgiver, the Redeemer, the Prince of Peace, who reigned in spiritual splendour from His Mansion of Delight and witnessed the early burgeoning of that Kingdom of God, the new heaven and the new earth, for the implanting of which in human hearts He had endured immeasurable and untold suffering and from which He had emerged victorious and resplendent to bequeath to humanity the virile and indestructible seed of a mighty tree for the sheltering and guarding of the unity of all on earth.

Chapter 19

THE ASCENSION OF BAHÁ'U'LLÁH

B AHÁ'U'LLÁH left this world on May 29th, 1892, eight hours after the sun had set the evening before. He had contracted a fever three weeks earlier which had mounted and declined and finally become acute. His last words to the weeping company, among them several pilgrims, whom He had summoned to His room in the Mansion, were spoken 'gently and affectionately':

I am very pleased with you all. Ye have rendered many services, and been very assiduous in your labours. Ye have come here every morning and every evening. May God assist you to remain united. May He aid you to exalt the Cause of the Lord of being![1]

He was laid to rest in a room of a house adjoining the Mansion. The shock to the Bahá'í world was immense and its grief indescribable. Nabíl attempted to portray the agony: 'Methinks, the spiritual commotion set up in the world of dust had caused all the worlds of God to tremble . . . My inner and outer tongue are powerless to portray the condition we were in . . . In the midst of the prevailing confusion a multitude of the inhabitants of 'Akká and of the neighbouring villages, that had thronged the fields surrounding the Mansion, could be seen weeping, beating their heads, and crying aloud their grief.'[2]

He found no consolation for his pain and drowned himself in the sea.

Shoghi Effendi relates:

For a full week a vast number of mourners, rich and poor alike, tarried to grieve with the bereaved family, partaking day and night of the food that was lavishly dispensed by its members. Notables, among whom were numbered Shí'ahs, Sunnís, Christians, Jews and Druzes, as well as poets, 'ulamás and government officials, all joined in lamenting the loss, and in magnifying the virtues and greatness of Bahá'u'lláh, many of them paying to Him their written tributes, in verse and in prose, in Arabic and Turkish. From cities as far afield as Damascus, Aleppo, Beirut and Cairo similar tributes were received.[3]

'The Sun of Bahá has set' were the opening words of the telegram sent to Sultán 'Abdu'l-Hamíd. Little did that monarch realize that although the earthly mission was accomplished, the sun of His world-encompassing influence was but rising above the horizon. The 'rolling up' of the old order would proceed throughout the twentieth century until the establishment of the Lesser Peace would open the way to the unification, regeneration and civilizing of all mankind.

The world treated Him as it has ever treated God's messenger, with enmity, hatred, scorn and persecution. He remained inviolate in His majesty to all the world could do, and responded with an outpouring of divine love and bountiful gifts of spiritual knowledge.

His life spanned the nineteenth century, when the great revolution in outlook and technique described in Chapter 2 led many to think that mankind was approaching a golden age. They were right, but gravely in error in their estimation of how it would come about and of its social and political arrangements. Very few recognized the hand of God at work in the world to fulfil His purpose in creating it. In spite of the universal adventism of the early years of the century, religion was declining and the general hope and vision of the future was of increasing material wealth and comfort. In the West this portended the dominance of European civilization and of European powers. Bahá'u'lláh knew how hollow were their attitudes and in urgent and compassionate warnings foretold the collapse of the 'lamentably defective' order of the world. Through its leaders, political and religious, He called the people to their true selves, to unity and brotherhood and the development of their spiritual natures. He wanted us to know and foster our 'best interests', rise to that station of spiritual nobility which would enable us to establish God's Kingdom on this earth and become qualified to inhabit it. He addressed every individual soul, expounding its reality, confirming the purpose of human life, and revealing innumerable prayers for its support. The Judge, the Lawgiver, the Redeemer, He taught us those things we could not bear in earlier times and opened upon us the floodgate of heaven's gifts. His prayers and meditations are replete with loving pleas for bounties and divine gifts to be showered upon us. Well aware of the human condition, He bequeathed to us a treasure house of prayers for assistance in our battle of life, for strengthening of spirit, for constancy, for relief from oppression, for health and happiness, for removal of difficulties, for knowledge and understanding and for drawing near to God. In one characteristic prayer, lamenting the persecutions endured by His followers, we find the following:

I implore Thee, O Thou Maker of the heavens and Lord of all names, by Thy most effulgent Self and Thy most exalted and all-glorious Remembrance, to send down upon Thy loved ones that which will draw them nearer unto Thee, and enable them to hearken unto Thine utterances . . . The doors of hope have been shut against the hearts that long for Thee, O my Lord! Their keys are in Thy hands; open them by the power of Thy might and Thy sovereignty. Potent art Thou to do as Thou pleasest. Thou art, verily, the Almighty, the Beneficent.

A recent statement, prepared at the request of the Universal House of Justice to mark the centenary in 1992 of Bahá'u'lláh's passing, contains in its foreword the following:

His vision of humanity as one people and of the earth as a common homeland, dismissed out of hand by the world leaders to whom it was first enunciated over a hundred years ago, has today become the focus of human hope.

This vision is clearly stated in two of Bahá'u'lláh's oft-quoted utterances:

The earth is but one country, and mankind its citizens.

Soon will the present-day order be rolled up, and a new one spread out in its stead.

And the Prince of Peace gave this assurance of the future of mankind:

These fruitless strifes, these ruinous wars shall pass away, and the 'Most Great Peace' shall come.

BIBLIOGRAPHY

'Abdu'l-Bahá. *'Abdu'l-Bahá in London*. Reprinted. Oakham: Bahá'í Publishing Trust, 1982.

—— *Memorials of the Faithful*. Translated by Marzieh Gail. Wilmette, Illinois: Bahá'í Publishing Trust, 1971.

—— *The Secret of Divine Civilization*. Translated from the original Persian text by Marzieh Gail. Wilmette, Illinois: Bahá'í Publishing Trust, 1957.

—— *Some Answered Questions*. Collected and translated from the Persian by Laura Clifford Barney. Wilmette, Illinois: Bahá'í Publishing Trust, 1981.

—— *A Traveller's Narrative*. Translated by Prof. Edward G. Browne. Wilmette, Illinois: Bahá'í Publishing Trust, rev. ed. 1980.

Bahá'í Prayers: A Selection of Prayers. Wilmette, Illinois: Bahá'í Publishing Trust, 1982.

Bahá'í Revelation: A Selection from the Bahá'í Holy Writings. London: Bahá'í Publishing Trust, 1955.

Bahá'u'lláh. *Epistle to the Son of the Wolf*. Wilmette, Illinois: Bahá'í Publishing Trust, 1962.

—— *Gleanings from the Writings of Bahá'u'lláh*. Translated by Shoghi Effendi. Wilmette, Illinois: Bahá'í Publishing Trust, 1963.

—— *The Hidden Words of Bahá'u'lláh*. Translated by Shoghi Effendi with the assistance of some English friends. Wilmette, Illinois: Bahá'í Publishing Trust, 1954.

—— *Kitáb-i-Íqán: The Book of Certitude*. Wilmette, Illinois: Bahá'í Publishing Trust, 1960.

—— *Prayers and Meditations*. Wilmette, Illinois: Bahá'í Publishing Trust, 1979.

—— *The Proclamation of Bahá'u'lláh to the Kings and Leaders of the World*. Compiled by the Universal House of Justice. Haifa: Bahá'í World Centre, 1967.

—— *Tablets of Bahá'u'lláh revealed after the Kitáb-i-Aqdas*. Compiled by the

Research Department of the Universal House of Justice and translated by Habib Taherzadeh with the assistance of a Committee at the Bahá'í World Centre. Haifa: Bahá'í World Centre, 1978.

Balyuzi, H. M. *The Báb: The Herald of the Day of Days*. Oxford: George Ronald, 1973.

Bahá'u'lláh, the King of Glory. Oxford: George Ronald, 1980.

Blomfield, Lady. *The Chosen Highway*. Wilmette, Illinois: Bahá'í Publishing Trust, 1967.

Curzon, George N. *Persia and the Persian Question*. London: Frank Cass and Co. Ltd., 1966.

Dorsey, Professor. *Why We Behave Like Human Beings*. New York: Harper Brothers.

Esslemont, J. E. *Bahá'u'lláh and the New Era*. Oakham: Bahá'í Publishing Trust, 4th rev. edn., 1976.

Hofman, David. *George Townshend*. Oxford: George Ronald, 1983.

Holy Bible. King James Version, 1911.

Maxwell, May. *An Early Pilgrimage*. rev. ed. Oxford: George Ronald, 1969.

Momen, Moojan. *The Bábí and Bahá'í Religions, 1844–1944: Some Contemporary Western Accounts*. Oxford: George Ronald, 1981.

—— *An Introduction to Shí'í Islam: The History and Doctrine of Twelver Shí'ism*. Oxford: George Ronald, 1985.

Nabíl-i-A'zam. *The Dawn-Breakers: Nabíl's Narrative of the Early Days of the Bahá'í Revelation*. Translated and edited by Shoghi Effendi. Wilmette, Illinois: Bahá'í Publishing Trust, 1974.

Priestly, J. B. *Literature and Western Man*. London: Heineman, 1960.

Seeking the Light of the Kingdom. Compilation issued by the Universal House of Justice. Oakham: Bahá'í Publishing Trust, 1977.

Shoghi Effendi. *God Passes By*. Wilmette, Illinois: Bahá'í Publishing Trust, 1944.

—— *The Promised Day is Come*. Wilmette, Illinois: Bahá'í Publishing Trust, 1961.

—— *The World Order of Bahá'u'lláh*. Wilmette, Illinois: Bahá'í Publishing Trust, 1969.

Star of the West. Reprinted in 8 volumes. Oxford: George Ronald, 1984.

Taherzadeh, Adib. *The Revelation of Bahá'u'lláh*. 4 vols. Oxford: George Ronald, 1974–87.

Townshend, George. *The Promise of All Ages*. Oxford: George Ronald, rev. ed. 1972.

The Universal House of Justice. *The Promise of World Peace*. Haifa: Bahá'í World Centre, 1985.

REFERENCES

INTRODUCTION

1. Bahá'u'lláh cited in *Proclamation*, p. v.
2. Shoghi Effendi, *God Passes By*, p. 94.
3. Bahá'u'lláh cited in *World Order of Bahá'u'lláh*, p. 113.

1. HOPE FOR MANKIND

1. Bahá'u'lláh, *Tablets*, p. 239.
2. Bahá'u'lláh cited in *World Order of Bahá'u'lláh*, p. 33.
3. ibid. p. 32.
4. Bahá'u'lláh, *Gleanings*, p. 7.
5. ibid. p. 286.
6. *'Abdu'l-Bahá in London*, p. 19.

2. THE NEW AGE

1. See Momen, *An Introduction to Shí'í Islam* and Balyuzi, *The Báb*.
2. Tennyson, *Locksley Hall*, lines 127–8.
3. Bahá'u'lláh, *Gleanings*, p. 200.
4. Bahá'u'lláh cited in *World Order of Bahá'u'lláh*, p. 33.
5. Browne in *Traveller's Narrative*.

3. THE BAHÁ'Í PEACE PROGRAMME

1. Bahá'u'lláh, *Gleanings*, p. 255.
2. *Seeking the Light of the Kingdom*, p. 5.
3. Bahá'u'lláh, *Gleanings*, p. 254.
4. ibid. p. 249.
5. 'Abdu'l-Bahá, *Secret of Divine Civilization*, pp. 64–5.
6. Shoghi Effendi, *World Order of Bahá'u'lláh*, p. 40.
7. ibid. p. 43.
8. The Universal House of Justice, *Promise*, p. 1.
9. ibid. p. 21.
10. Bahá'u'lláh, *Gleanings*, p. 136.

11. 'Abdu'l-Bahá cited in *World Order of Bahá'u'lláh*, p. 169.
12. Shoghi Effendi, *World Order of Bahá'u'lláh*, p. 43.
13. Bahá'u'lláh, *Tablets*, p. 35.
14. 'Abdu'l-Bahá, 'Tablet to the Hague', *Bahá'í Revelation*, pp. 208–19.
15. Bahá'u'lláh, *Tablets*, p. 68.
16. Bahá'u'lláh, *Gleanings*, pp. 99–100.
17. ibid. p. 200.
18. Bahá'u'lláh, *Tablets*, pp. 63–4.
19. 'Abdu'l-Bahá, *Promulgation*, p. 171.
20. Dorsey, *Why We Behave*.
21. Townshend, *Promise of All Ages*, pp. 31–2.
22. Bahá'u'lláh, *Gleanings*, p. 288.
23. Bahá'u'lláh, *Íqán*, p. 98.
24. *Bahá'í Prayers*, p. 122.
25. Bahá'u'lláh, *Íqán*, pp. 99–100.
26. ibid. pp. 152–4.
27. Bahá'u'lláh, *Gleanings*, p. 217.
28. ibid. p. 95.
29. Priestly, *Literature*.
30. Bahá'u'lláh, *Gleanings*, p. 215.
31. ibid. p. 287.
32. Bahá'u'lláh, *Hidden Words*, Arabic nos. 3, 4, 5, 8, 13, 15, 32; Persian no. 70.
33. Shoghi Effendi, *World Order of Bahá'u'lláh*, pp. 202–4.

4. THE NEW REVELATION

1. Nabíl-i-A'ẓam, *Dawn-Breakers*.
2. See Hofman, *George Townshend*, p. 114.
3. The Báb cited in *Dawn-Breakers*, p. 96.

5. THE NOBLEMAN OF NÚR

1. Shoghi Effendi, *God Passes By*, p. 94.
2. Nabíl-i-A'ẓam, *Dawn-Breakers*, pp. 119–20.
3. Esslemont, *New Era*, pp. 23–4.
4. Nabíl-i-A'ẓam, *Dawn-Breakers*, pp. 117–8.
5. ibid. pp. 104–8

6. MÍRZÁ ḤUSAYN 'ALÍ, THE BÁBÍ

1. Shoghi Effendi, *God Passes By*, p. 37.
2. Bahá'u'lláh, *Epistle*, p. 20.
3. Bahíyyih Khanum cited in *Chosen Highway*, pp. 40–1.

7. PRISONER IN THE SÍYÁH-CHÁL

1. Bahá'u'lláh, *Epistle*, pp. 20–1.
2. ibid. p. 77.
3. Nabíl-i-A'zam, *Dawn-Breakers*, p. 461.
4. Talk given by 'Abdu'l-Bahá in Los Angeles, 19 October 1912. *Star of the West*, vol. VII.
5. Bahá'u'lláh, *Epistle*, p. 22.
6. ibid. p. 21.
7. Bahá'u'lláh cited in *God Passes By*, pp. 101–2.

8. EXILE

1. Shoghi Effendi, *God Passes By*, p. 105.
2. ibid. p. 108.
3. Bahá'u'lláh cited in ibid. p. 109.
4. ibid. p. 103.
5. See *Dawn-Breakers*, p. 372.

9. DARVÍSH MUḤAMMAD-I-ÍRÁNÍ

1. Bahá'u'lláh, *Íqán*, p. 251.
2. Shoghi Effendi, *God Passes By*, p. 120.
3. Nabíl-i-A'zam, *Dawn-Breakers*, p. 585.
4. Balyuzi, *King of Glory*, p. 117.
5. ibid. p. 116.
6. Shoghi Effendi, *God Passes By*, p. 120.
7. Bahá'u'lláh, *Íqán*, p. 250.
8. ibid. pp. 250–1.
9. Shoghi Effendi, *God Passes By*, p. 120.
10. ibid. p. 121.
11. ibid. p. 122.
12. ibid. pp. 123–4.
13. 'Abdu'l-Bahá cited in ibid. p. 124.
14. Shoghi Effendi, *God Passes By*, p. 121.

10. RETURN TO BAGHDAD

1. Balyuzi, *King of Glory*, p. 122.
2. Shoghi Effendi, *God Passes By*, pp. 129–31.
3. ibid. pp. 134–5.
4. ibid. p. 135.
5. Shoghi Effendi, *God Passes By*, pp. 135–6.
6. ibid. p. 141.

7. ibid. p. 143.
8. ibid. p. 144.
9. 'Abdu'l-Bahá, *Some Answered Questions*, chapter 9.
10. Balyuzi, *King of Glory*, p. 145.
11. 'Abdu'l-Bahá, *Some Answered Questions*, p. 35.
12. Balyuzi, *King of Glory*, p. 155.
13. Shoghi Effendi, *God Passes By*, p. 148.
14. ibid. p. 149.
15. ibid.
16. ibid. pp. 149–50.
17. ibid. p. 150.

11. BAHÁ'U'LLÁH'S DECLARATION OF HIS MISSION

1. Shoghi Effendi, *God Passes By*, p. 144.
2. ibid. p. 152.
3. ibid. pp. 152–3.
4. Nabíl cited in ibid. p. 153.
5. Bahá'u'lláh, *Gleanings*, pp. 35, 30, 31, 5, 10–11, 11, 6–7, Tablet of Aḥmad.
6. Shoghi Effendi, *God Passes By*, p. 155.
7. ibid.

12. BY CARAVAN TO CONSTANTINOPLE

1. Shoghi Effendi, *God Passes By*, p. 156.
2. Balyuzi, *King of Glory*, pp. 187–8.
3. 'Abdu'l-Bahá, *Memorials*, p. 146.

14. THE PROCLAMATION TO THE KINGS AND RELIGIOUS LEADERS

1. Shoghi Effendi, *God Passes By*, p. 172.
2. Bahá'u'lláh cited in ibid. p. 181.
3. Bahá'u'lláh cited in *Promised Day is Come*, p. 62,
4. ibid. p. 52.
5. Bahá'u'lláh, *Epistle*, pp. 50–1.
6. Shoghi Effendi, *God Passes By*, p. 199.
7. Bahá'u'lláh cited in ibid. p. 197.
8. Shoghi Effendi, *Promised Day is Come*, p. 66.
9. Bahá'u'lláh, *Gleanings*, pp. 246–7.
10. Bahá'u'lláh cited in *World Order of Bahá'u'lláh*, p. 104.
11. Balyuzi, *King of Glory*, p. 15.

12. Bahá'u'lláh, *Tablets*, p. 24.
13. Shoghi Effendi, *God Passes By*, p. 230.

15. ADRIANOPLE AND THE LAST BANISHMENT

1. Shoghi Effendi, *God Passes By*, p. 166.
2. ibid. p. 169.
3. ibid. p. 170.
4. Curzon, *Persia*.
5. Balyuzi, *King of Glory*, p. 220.
6. ibid. p. 221.
7. ibid. p. 222.
8. ibid. p. 243.
9. Shoghi Effendi, *God Passes By*, p. 177.
10. ibid. p. 180.
11. E.G. Browne cited in *Traveller's Narrative*.
12. Balyuzi, *King of Glory*, p. 259.
13. ibid. p. 256.
14. Shoghi Effendi, *God Passes By*, pp. 179–81.
15. ibid. p. 182.
16. Balyuzi, *King of Glory*, pp. 267–8.

16. 'AKKÁ, THE MOST GREAT PRISON

1. Isa. 2:2–3; 40:9–10; 9:6–7; Ps. 24:9–10; Amos 1:2.
2. Shoghi Effendi, *God Passes By*, p. 184.
3. Bahá'u'lláh cited in ibid.
4. Bahá'u'lláh cited in ibid. p. 185.
5. Bahá'u'lláh, *Gleanings*, p. 136.
6. Bahá'u'llah cited in *World Order of Bahá'u'lláh*, p. 109.
7. Bahá'u'lláh cited in *God Passes By*, p. 186.
8. ibid. p. 188.
9. ibid.
10. ibid.
11. ibid. p. 189.
12. Balyuzi, *King of Glory*, p. 326.
13. ibid.
14. ibid. p. 327.
15. Shoghi Effendi, *God Passes By*, p. 190.
16. ibid.
17. ibid. pp. 190–1.
18. ibid. p. 190.
19. ibid. p. 191.

20. ibid. p. 213.
21. ibid. pp. 217–8.
22. ibid. p. 192.

17. FREEDOM

1. Bahá'u'lláh cited in *King of Glory*, p. 360.
2. 'Abdu'l-Bahá cited in ibid. pp. 357–9.

18. BAHJÍ – THE FINAL YEARS

1. Bahá'u'lláh cited in *God Passes By*, p. 196.
2. 'Abdu'l-Bahá cited in ibid.
3. ibid., p. 193.
4. Ṭúbá <u>Kh</u>ánum cited in *Chosen Highway*, p. 97.
5. Maxwell, *Early Pilgrimage*, pp. 33–4.
6. Esslemont, *New Era*, p. 36.

19. THE ASCENSION OF BAHÁ'U'LLÁH

1. Bahá'u'lláh cited in *God Passes By*, p. 222.
2. Nabíl cited in ibid.
3. Shoghi Effendi, *God Passes By*, pp. 222–3.

INDEX

'Abdu'l-Ázíz, Sulṭán 80, 103–4
  addressed in *Súriy-i-Mulúk* and
    verbal messages, 107
  issues decree of fourth
    banishment, 140
  punishment, 111–12
'Abdu'l-Bahá
  addresses Socialists, 24
  announces new age in City
    Temple, 4
  appointed Centre of the
    Covenant, 177
  in Baghdad, 68
  describes Bahá'u'lláh to
    Esslemont, 43–4
  effect on Governor of 'Akká, 152
  imprisoned in 'Akká, 160
  on journey to Constantinople, 96
  leadership of Bahá'í community,
    162, 165, 176
  Most Great Branch, 177
  perpetuates Covenant, 177
  recounts story of Bahá'u'lláh
    leaving 'Akká, 167–8
  sees Bahá'u'lláh in Síyáh-Chál,
    54
  station of, 139
  work in 'Akká effecting
    transformation in fortunes
    of Faith, 161–3
'Abdu'l-Ghaffár, 145
'Abdu'l-Husayn, Shaykh, *see*
  Shaykh 'Abdu'l-Husayn

'Abdu'l-Majíd, Sulṭán, 80
abomination of desolations, 8
Abraham, 27, 39, 41, 128
Abu'l-Faḍl, Mírzá, 149
Abu'l-Qásim, 65, 68
Abu'l-Qásim, the gardener, 171
Adrianople, *chapter 15*, 90
  arrival of exiles, 102
  Governor of, and diplomats
    distressed at fourth
    banishment, 141
  greatest crisis, 105
  zenith of ministry, 105
Aḥmad Big Tawfíq, Governor of
  'Akká
  farewell party by Bahá'ís, 163
  repairs aqueduct, 162–3
  sends son to 'Abdu'l-Bahá for
    instruction, 162
  treats exiles with justice, 162
'Akká, *chapter 16*, 66, 90, 140–1
  arrival in, 149–51
  climate, 149, 163
  description by Bahá'u'lláh, 154
  improvement of conditions, 157
  journey from Adrianople to,
    141–5, 149–55
  Most Great Prison, 151–4
  populace, 150
  references in scripture to, 148–9
  strict conditions, 154–5
Alexander, 96
Alexander II, Czar, 118–19

Alexandria, Nabíl's imprisonment in, 143–4
'Alí Big, 136–7
'Alí Páshá, 80–1, 99, 100
  receives condemnatory letter, 103
Alláh-u-Akbar, 90
America, 122
Amru'llah, House of, 137–8
Anatolia, *chapter 12*, 82, 92
antichrist of Bahá'í revelation, 62
  see also Muḥammad, Siyyid
Áqá Ján Big, murdered in 'Akká, 159
Áqáy-i-Kalím, *see* Mízrá Músá
Ascension of Bahá'u'lláh, *chapter 19*
Áshchí, Áqá Ḥusayn-i-, 95, 137, 138
  marries, 151
Ásíyih Khánum, *see* Navváb
attempt on the life of the Shah, 49–50
Austria, Emperor of, 119

Báb, the, 37–40
  opposition and death, 38
  remains of, transferred, 139
  site of Shrine, 173–4
Bábís
  Bahá'u'lláh resolves to regenerate, 62
  declined to desperate condition, 62, 70–1
  holocaust against, 52
  regenerated by Bahá'u'lláh, 62–3
  transformed to Bahá'ís, 90
  Turkish government withdraws protection, 140
Badí', 118
Baghdad, *chapters 8 and 10*
  centre of civilization, 27
  departure from, 90–1, 93

preparation for, 80–2
  tumultuous scenes, weeping crowds, 83–4, 90–1
Bahá'í Faith
  Administration, 177
  defence, 2
  dispersion, xiv
  emerges onto world stage, 1
  persecution of, 1–2
  spiritual power, 2, 4
  spread of, 139
  transformation in fortunes, 161
Bahá'í, individual, 30–1
Bahá'í Peace Programme, *chapter 3*, 20
Bahá'í World Centre, 146
Bahá'u'lláh
  acquires Turkish citizenship, 73
  advises Prime Minister, 58
  ancestry, 41
  anger at unjust edict, 101
  appoints 'Abdu'l-Bahá His successor, Centre of the Covenant, 177
  apotheosis, xii, 54–6
  arrested and questioned, 159–61
  arrested and taken to Síyáh-Chál, 50–1
  ascendancy, 67–8
  Ascension, *chapter 19*
  attempts to assassinate, 73, 131–2
  attends Ramadan feast at Government House, 138
  banishments
    Adrianople, 101
    'Akká, 140
    Baghdad, 58
    Constantinople, 80
  becomes a Bábí, 47
  birth, 41
  calligraphy, 66–7

challenges 'ulamá, 78–9
childhood, 42–3
comment on Tablet to Grand
    Vizier, 103–4
comparison with previous
    Manifestations, xiii-xiv,
    54–5, 64
compassion and love, 73
compassion for mankind, 22–3,
    179
Conference of Badasht, presides
    at, 48–9
Darvísh Muhammad-i-Íraní,
    64–9
Declaration, chapter 11
description, frontispiece
distress at Yahyá's conduct, 132
distress over murder, 161
edict of third banishment, 101–2
enmity of Persian ambassador,
    100–1
expels members of community,
    158–9
family name (Buzurg), 41–2
father's dream, 42–3
frustrates plan of unfriendly
    Governor, 164–5
gives His prayer rug for money to
    bury friends, 154
gives Tablet to every individual
    believer, 81–2
'He Whom God shall make
    manifest', 38, 39, 61, 93
His cell in Most Great Prison,
    155–6
His life in Baghdad, 71–2, 73–5
House in Baghdad, 74
House surrounded by soldiers,
    140
import of arrival in 'Akká,
    151–2

imprisonment, chapter 7, xiii,
    50–1
incident of stolen mules, 94–5
'inner radiance' appeared after
    Síyáh-Chál, 61
interviews Browne, 9
introduced, 1
journey to Adrianople, 102
journeys of exile
    to Adrianople, 102
    to 'Akká, 141–5
    Baghdad to Constantinople,
        chapter 12
    Teheran to Baghdad, 58–60
leaves 'Akká, 167–8
letter to Persian ambassador,
    102–3
lives at Mazra'ih, 170
majesty, 67, 150, 152–3, 160,
    161
Manifestation of God, xii
marriage, 44–5
meditation upon decree of God,
    59–60
monarchs addressed individually,
    107
    see also individual names
moral grandeur, 63
offers forgiveness to Mírzá
    Yahyá, 133
peace and honour in last days,
    166
points out site of the Báb's
    Shrine, 174
popular enthusiasm, 90–1
power to reconcile enemies, 73
proclaims station and mission to
    world's leaders, chapter 14
Promised One of all ages, xii, 3,
    38, 88, 93
promotes new revelation,
    chapter 6

rebellion of Yaḥyá, 130–4
receives letter from the Báb, 46
reception in capital, 99–100
regenerates Bábí community,
    63, 70–2
relationship to family, 166
released from Síyáh-Chál, 57–8
requests Governor to repair
    aqueduct, 162–3
requests Shah to call conference
    of divines for Him to
    address, 117
retires to Kurdistan, *chapter 9*
    becomes revered and loved, 68
returns to Baghdad, *chapter 10*
reveals *Epistle to the Son of the
    Wolf*, 177–8
reveals healing prayer, 154
royal progress to Constantinople,
    92–8
suffers imprisonment and
    bastinado, 22, 47
Súriy-i-Mulúk, 107–10
teaching revolutionary, xi
titles of:
    Blessed Perfection, 142
    Judge, 178
    King of Kings, xiv, 178
    Law-giver, 178
    Lord of Hosts, xii, xiv, 3, 93,
        147, 178
    Prince of Peace, xiv, 178
    Redeemer, 147, 178
treatment of Yaḥyá, 62–3
victory over enemies, 169–70
warns friends of future hardships,
    142
writings after *Aqdas*, 165
writings from Bahjí, 176–7
Bahíyyih Khánum, 59, 150
    relates story of Bahá'u'lláh's
        arrest, 50–1

story of schoolboy in
    Sulaymáníyyih, 66–7
tells of 'inner radiance' of
    Bahá'u'lláh, 61
Bahjí, Mansion of, 172–3, 176
    inscription over entrance, 178
    Shrine of Bahá'u'lláh, 178
Balfour Declaration, 146
Balyuzi, H.M., Hand of the Cause,
    Acknowledgements
    portrays Bahá'ís in Adrianople,
        136
Bible, 146–8
    prophecies in *Deuteronomy*, 146
Blomfield, Lady, 50–1, 66
Browne, Professor E.G., quoted
    frontispiece
    meets Bahá'u'lláh, 9, 173
Buddha, xii, 4, 27
Burns, Robert, 6
Buzurg, family name of
    Bahá'u'lláh, 41–2

Carlyle, 6
Carmel, Mount, 146, 156
    visited by Bahá'u'lláh, 173–4
    site of the Báb's Shrine, 174
    Tablet of, 174–6
Caspian Sea, 42
Chosen Highway, The, 51, 66
Christ, *see* Jesus
Christendom, priests of, addressed,
    125–7
City Temple, London, 4
collective security, 11–12
companions
    accompany Bahá'u'lláh from
        Baghdad, 92
    in Adrianople, on third exile,
        chapter 23
    dispersion on fourth banishment,
        142

enter Most Great Prison, 153–4
Persian ambassador advises all
     consuls protection of
     Turkey withdrawn, 140
sufferings on sail across Bay of
     Haifa, 149–50
compassion, 22, 178
Conference of Bada_sh_t, 48–9
Constantinople
     'Abdu'l-'Azíz decrees third
          banishment, 101–2
     see also Adrianople
     arrival, 99
     corruption of court, 100
     enmity of Persian ambassador,
          100–1
     invitation from Sultan, 80–1
     journey from Baghdad, chapter 12
Covenant, 177
Crusades, 149
Curzon, Lord, 41–2, 48
Cyprus, 140, 158
Czar Alexander II, 118–19

Daniel the prophet, 8
Dark Ages, 70
Darví_sh_ Muḥammad-i-Írání,
     chapter 9
Darví_sh_ Muṣṭafá, 44
Day of God, chapter 11, 8, 38, 39
Declaration in Garden of Riḍván,
     chapter 11, 82–3
     not public, 106
Deuteronomy, 146
Dolgorouki, Prince, assists
     Bahá'u'lláh, 50, 58

Edirne, see Adrianople
Edict of Toleration, 146
education, 20–1
Episode of the Báb, chapter 4
Epistle to the Son of the Wolf, 177

Esslemont, Dr J.E., 43–4, 172–3

false priests, 30
false prophets, 30
Fáris, 143–4
Fast, 138, 139
first effulgence, 18–19
French Revolution, 6, 7
Fry, Elizabeth, 7
Fu'ád Pá_sh_á, 99, 140
fundamentalist, 31

Gabriel, xiv
Gallipoli, 141–2
Garden of Riḍván, chapter 11
     Declaration in, not public, 106
Garden of Riḍván, Na'mayn,
     170–2
     stories of, 171–2
German Templers, 149, 173
God, xii
     purpose of, 31–2
     transcendence, 25–6
'God of the Persians', 150

Haifa, 149
     dominant feature, 174
Hasan-i-'Ammú (Ḥájí), 78–9
Hebrew Prophets, 146–8
'He Whom God shall make
     manifest', see Bahá'u'lláh
     claimants, 61–2
     declared, 82
Hidden Words, The, 32–3, 66
Hindus, xii
Hohenzollern, 114–15
Holy Spirit, 32
House of 'Abbúd, 157, 163
House of 'Údí _Kh_ammár, 157
humanity
     coming of age, 2
     oneness of, 21–5, 30, 36

unity of, 3–4, 15, 17, 21–5, 30,
    33–6
Ḥusayn, Mullá, 39–40, 45–6
Ḥusayn Khán Mírzá, 155

international authority, *chapter 3*
international language, 20
Iran, *see* Persia
Iraq, 48
    see also Baghdad
Isaiah, 147
Ishráqát, Tablet of, 171–2
Islam
    great civilization, 37
    ignorant clergy, 42
    opposition to Bahá'u'lláh, 72–3
    Shi'ah-Sunni, 58
Ismá'íl, Shaykh, 67

Ja'far-i-Tabrízí, Hájí, 140–1
Ján Big, Áqá, 159
Jesse, 41
Jesus, xiv, 4, 8, 18, 27, 30, 39
Jews, addressed, 124, 146–8
Judaism, chief priests of, 128

Kabrí Springs, 162
Kaiser Wilhelm I, 114–15
Kalím, Áqáy-i-, *see* Mírzá Músá
Karbila, 48, 76, 77
Karkúk, 96–7
Kazimayn, 76, 77
Kemball, Sir Arnold Burrows,
    British Consul-General in
    Baghdad, offers Bahá'u'lláh
    British citizenship, 72
Khartoum, 140
Khurshíd Páshá, Governor of
    Adrianople, 138
    devoted to Bahá'u'lláh and
    'Abdu'l-Bahá, 138
Kingdom of God, 10, 147–8, 151

kings, addressed, *chapter 14*
    'drunk with pride', 129
    power of, 112
kingship, 129
Kitáb-i-Aqdas, 107
    described by Shoghi Effendi,
        163–4, 165
    revealed in 'Akká, 163
Kitáb-i-Íqán, 29, 66, 69
knowledge of God, xiii
Krishna, xii, 4, 27

language, 20
League of Nations, 7, 13
Lesser Peace, *chapter 3*
Letters of the Living, 38–9
Lincoln, Abraham, 7
literacy, 20
locusts, story of, 171
Lord of Hosts, *see* Bahá'u'lláh
love, 32–3

Maḥmúd, Mírzá, 137
Maiden, 55, 171–2
man, spiritual being, 4
    did not create himself, 25
    knows himself, 18–19
    oneness of, *chapter 3*
Manifestation of God, the, xii–xiv
    accepts vicissitudes of human
        life, 133
    compassion of, 133
    inspires onward movement of
        mankind, 25–7
    source of civilization, 4
    source of spiritual knowledge, 25
    two natures, 28–9
Mardin, 94–5
Marie, Queen, 170
martyrs and martyrdom, 38, 50
Matthew, St, 8
Maxwell, May, 170–1

Mázindarán, 42
Mazra'ih, 170
McNeill, General, 170
Memorials of the Faithful, 145
Messiah, 149
Middle East, 37
Mihdí, Mírzá, *see* Mírzá Mihdí
Mírzá Abu'l-Faḍl, 149
Mírzá Ḥusayn Khán, 155
Mírzá Maḥmúd, 137
Mírzá Mihdí
    death of, 156–7
    funeral, 157
    interred on Mount Carmel, 157
    relationship to Father, 166
Mírzá Muḥammad-Qulí, 59
Mírzá Músá, 46
    helps Navváb, 51, 59
    sends mission to Bahá'u'lláh in
        Sulaymáníyyih, 68
Mírzá Yaḥyá
    appointed by the Báb, 61
    campaign against Bahá'u'lláh,
        63, 130–2
    challenges Bahá'u'lláh, 132
    character, 61, 130
    cowardly attitude in
        Constantinople, 101–2
    damage to Faith, 133–4
    educated by Bahá'u'lláh, 62
    effect on Bábí community, 70,
        85, 133–4
    expelled, 132
    goes into hiding, 61, 62–3
    joins caravan at Mosul, 95–6
    misled by Siyyid Muḥammad, 62
    saved from bastinado, 62
Mishkín-Qalam, 137
monks, pious deeds, 128
monotheism, 27
Monument Garden, 157
Moses, xiv, 4, 27, 39, 128

Most Great Peace, *chapter 3*, xi, 9,
    36
Most Great Prison, *see*, 'Akká
Muhammad, xiii, 4, 27, 39, 66, 128
Muḥammad Ustád, 131–2, 137
Muḥammad-i-Iṣfáhání, Siyyid, *see*
    Siyyid Muḥammad-i-
    Iṣfáhání
Muḥammad-Qulí, Mírzá, 59
Muḥammad Taqí, Shaykh, 177–8
Mulla (Ḥájí) Ḥasan-i-'Ammú, 78–9
Mullá Ḥusayn, 39–40
    finds Bahá'u'lláh, 45–6
    mission to Teheran, 45–6
    murder in 'Akká, 157–61
Murtiḍáy-i-Anṣárí, Shaykh, 78
Músá, Mírzá, *see* Mírzá Músá
Muṣṭafá, Darvísh, 44
mysticism, 32

Nabíl-i-A'ẓam, 38, 44, 69, 137,
    139
    drowns himself, 179
    incident at Alexandria, 143–4
Najaf, 76, 77
Najíb Páshá, 82
Najíbíyyih Garden, 82–3
Námiq Páshá, 76, 84, 93
Napoleon, 149
Napoleon III, 112–14
Náṣiri'd-Dín Sháh, 83–4, 117–18
Navváb
    death, 52
    grief-stricken and consoled by
        Bahá'u'lláh, 166
    maintains family while
        Bahá'u'lláh is in Síyáh-
        Chál, 51–2
    marries Bahá'u'lláh, 44–5
    tomb on Mount Carmel, 52
    welcomes Bahá'u'lláh after
        release from Síyáh-Chál, 58

Naw-Rúz, 81
new age, *chapter 2*, 153
New World Order, *chapter 3*
Nimrod, 39
nineteenth century, 6
Núr, *chapter 5*

order, rolled up, 3, 182

parliaments, addressed, 120–1
peace, *chapter 3*, 1, 3–4
  two stages, 10
  see also Lesser Peace *and* Most
    Great Peace
Persia, 6, 41–2
  nobility of, 41
Pharisees, 128
Pharaoh, 39, 128
pilgrims to 'Akká, 155–6
pilgrims' notes, 171
Pilgrimage, 139–40
  made excuse by enemies, 139–40
Pope Pius IX, 115–17
priests, *see* religious leaders
priesthood, abolished, 128
Priestley, J.B., 31
proclamation of Bahá'u'lláh's
  mission, *chapter 14*
Promise of World Peace, The, 14
Promised Day, 3
Promised One of All Ages, 3, 88,
  89
prophecy, fulfilment of, 88, 146–8
  Isaiah's prophecy about Prince of
    Peace, 147–8
Ptolemais, 149
  see also 'Akká
Purest Branch, *see* Mírzá Mihdí

Qá'im, 149
Qajars, 118
Queen Marie, 170

Queen Victoria, 119–22
  prayer for, 121–2, 129
  Tablet to, 10, 11–12, 119–21
Qur'án, 46

red roan stallion, 90–1
religion
  decline of, 8, 9, 123–4
  gives most satisfying picture of
    universe, 31
  harmony with science, 23
  importance of, 23–4
religious leaders
  always opposed to new message,
    127–8
  attempts to hold back
    knowledge, 31
  deprived of power, 128–9
  fall of, 115–17
  idolatrous, 128
  power of, 112
Richard Lionheart, 149
Ridá, Áqá, 97, 152, 159–60
Ridván, Festival of, 82
Ridván, Garden of, 82
Ridván, ninth day of, 90
romantic movement, 6–7

Sálih, 157
Samsun, 82, 97
science
  harmony with religion, 23
  cannot create peace, 24
Sedan, battle of, 114
Seven Valleys, The, 66
Shaftesbury, 7
Shah, xiii
Sháh-Bahrám, xii
Shamsí Big, 103
Shaykh 'Abdu'l-Husayn, 76–9
  attempts to extradite
    Bahá'u'lláh, 76, 77

plans holy war against Bábís, 77–8
demands miracle from Bahá'u'lláh, 78–9
Shaykh Ismá'íl, 67
Shaykh Muhammad-Taqí, Son of the Wolf, 177–8
Shaykh Murtidáy-i-Ansárí, 78
Shaykh Sultán, 68–9, 70
Shaykhi movement, 6
Shi'ah Islam, xii
 corrupt clergy, 49
 persecuted the Báb, 128
 priests addressed, 127
 stronghold in Iraq, 76
Shiraz, 37
Shrine of the Báb, Queen of Carmel, 174
Síyáh-Chál, chapter 7, xii, 50, 51
 promise of 'treasure' fulfilled, 139
Siyyid Muhammad-i-Isfáhání, antichrist of Bahá'í revelation, 62
 activities in 'Akká, 157–9
 character, 130
 damage to Faith, 133
 dominates Yahyá, 62
 effect on Bábí community, 70
 murdered in 'Akká, 159
 sets out to destroy Bahá'u'lláh, 63, 130
slavery, abolished, 7
Some Answered Questions, 29
soul of man, 21
Statue of Liberty, 122–3
Sublime Porte, 79, 107
Sulaymáníyyih, chapter 9
Sultán, Shaykh, 68–9, 70
Sultans, see by name
Sun of Truth, 28
Sunni Islam, xii

priests addressed, 127
Súriy-i-Amr, 132
Súriy-i-Mulúk, 107–10
Súriy-i-Ra'ís, 111, 141

Tablet of Ahmad, 134–6
Tablet of the Branch, 139
Tablet of Carmel, 174–6
Tablet of the Holy Mariner, 81
Tablet of Tarázát, 171
Tabriz, 38
Taherzadeh, Adib, 150
Táhirih, 49
Teheran, 39–40, 45–6
telegram, first sent, 7, 37
Templers, German, 149, 173
Tennyson, Alfred Lord, 7
time, foretold, 8
Townshend, Archdeacon George, 148n
Toynbee, Professor Arnold, 24
Traveller's Narrative, A, 9
trustworthiness, 171–2
Turkish government
 Edict of Toleration to Jews, 146
 withdraws protection from Bábís, 140

'Údí Khammár, 157, 172
Unfoldment of World Civilization, The, 33–5
ungodliness, 8
United Nations, 15, 16
unities, three, 21–2
Universal House of Justice, 14, 15
Ustád Muhammad, 131–2, 137

Victoria, Queen, see Queen Victoria

Wilberforce, 7
William I, Kaiser, 114–15
Wilson, Woodrow, 7

women, equality of sexes, 22–3
Word of God, 28
Words of Paradise, 21
world economy, 19–20
World Order, 2–3, 21, 177
    birth pangs, 3, 9
world mythology, 36

worship, 28

Yaḥyá, Mírzá, *see* Mírzá Yaḥya

Zoraster, 4, 27
Zoroastrians, xii
    addressed, 125